MS. MURDER

Volume I
Edited by Marie Smith

The detectives in these stories are shrewd, sophisticated, even hard-boiled. Amateur or professional, they unravel mysteries that involve the reader right from the start. From the French Riviera to St Mary Mead, England; from exotic Havana to the privileged world of the British aristocracy, Ms. Murder presents the best by the best.

MS. MURDER

The Best Mysteries

Featuring Women Detectives, By The Top Women Writers
Volume I

Edited by
MARIE SMITH

Curley Publishing, Inc.
South Yarmouth, Ma.

Library of Congress Cataloging-in-Publication Data

Ms. Murder: the best mysteries featuring women detectives, by the top
  women writers / edited by Marie Smith.
   p. cm.
  1. Detective and mystery stories, American—Women authors.
  2. Detective and mystery stories, English—Women authors.
  3. American fiction—20th century. 4. English fiction—20th
  century. 5. Women detectives—Fiction. 6. Large type books.
  I. Smith, Marie.
  [PS648.D4M7 1990]
  813'.0108352042—dc20
  ISBN 0–7927–0582–3 (v. 1: lg. print)   90–35792
  ISBN 0–7927–0583–1 (v. 1: pbk.: lg. print)   CIP

Published in Large Print by arrangement with Carol
Publishing Group in the United States and Canada, along
with Xanadu Publications Ltd. in the U.K. and British
Commonwealth.

Distributed in Great Britain, Ireland and the
Commonwealth by CHIVERS LIBRARY SERVICES
LIMITED, Bath BA1 3HB, England.

Printed in Great Britain

Contents

Introduction

A recent poll of mystery readers revealed that their three favourite authors are, first, Agatha Christie, second, Dorothy L. Sayers and, third, Margery Allingham. Clearly, this is one area of human endeavour where women are *not* second-class citizens, and the recent sale of the publishing rights to Agatha Christie's books for an advance payment of ninety-three million dollars suggests that publishers wouldn't quarrel with the readers' assessment: that women write very good mysteries.

What is perhaps more significant is that until very recently they have been writing mostly about men. One could argue, I suppose, that since most detectives *are* men this is only to be expected, but if one views the mystery story as a sort of modern morality play – on •the whole I concur with W. H. Auden's insightful analysis of the form – then it begins to seem strange.

Since W. S. Hayward's *The Revelations of a Lady Detective*, who pre-dates the arrival of Sherlock Holmes by a couple of decades, there have always been female sleuths in fiction, of course; the early ones have been ably chronicled by Michele B. Slung in her collection *Crime on her Mind*, which is an amusing gallery of Victorian and Edwardian gels who did a bit of detecting now and again and generally ended up in the arms of their betrothed; while post-Sherlock, the female characters in mystery stories tended to fall into certain stock types. There was the Plucky Girl Detective exemplified by Nancy Drew and dozens like her, the Lady in Distress of a thousand Gothics and the entire 'Had-I-But-Known' school, the Meddling Old Spinster, the Whacky Wife (Mrs North, Helen Justus, Nora Charles and so on), and the Hardboiled Heroine who drank, swore and toted a gun just like Sam Spade – not to mention all the doting girlfriends, worried wives and comic charladies. One looks mostly in vain for a female character who isn't a cliché, and it leaves one wondering how things have fared since then.

The present collection may be said to take up where Ms Slung left off, and it aims informally to chart the progress of the female sleuth from Edwardian times to the present. It is heartening to see how things *have* changed, and it is women writers who have largely brought the change about.

In the first story in this book, Solange Fontaine says that 'the height of femininity is an acutely enhanced passivity. The women who made history, the Helens and the Cleopatras, didn't go out and do things, they just lay about and things happened.' Solange herself does not do much but has a 'feeling' for evil which enables her to solve crimes. (A few years later, feminine intuition was banned from mystery stories in the rules of the Detection Club.) Yet in other ways Solange was a pioneer, an independent young woman who at the end of the series rejected *both* her suitors to concentrate on her profession.

It was a long time before this ground was regained, in life and in the mystery story. In between we find a host of the sort of stock characters that I detailed earlier, from which I have had to select very carefully. There are several elderly spinsters in the pages that follow, but they are the more interesting ones like Miss Marple and the redoubtable Mrs (later Dame) Beatrice Lestrange Bradley; there's also one whacky wife and a few ladies in distress, including Nurse Susan Dare, but they are I think more believable than most – young women who aren't detectives at all except in so far as events force them to be.

There are one or two authors that I regret not being able to include in this book, especially Margery Allingham and P. D. James, but alas the former never wrote about a female detective and the latter's admirable Cordelia Grey exists only in a novel, *An Unsuitable Job for a Woman*. Otherwise, my guiding principle has been less to select rigidly 'representative' stories from all the phases in the development of the female detective, which could easily have become tedious, than simply to try and choose good ones.

MARIE SMITH
Dorset, 1989

F. TENNYSON JESSE

Solange Fontaine in
The Lover of St Lys

It was in a little grey town set high in the mountainous country behind the Riviera that Solange and her father decided to spend their summer holiday. St. Lys, seen once on a motor-tour, had enraptured them both – a town of mellow, fluted tiles, of grey walls, of steep streets that were shadowed ways of coolness even at noonday, and ramparts that circled round the mountain crest as though hacked out of the living rock, so sheer and straight they were. It was a restful place, the very townspeople, with their clear, dark eyes and rough-hewn faces, strong of jaw and cheekbone, tender with pure skins and creamy colours, seemed redolent of peace. Here was a town for tired workers, especially for workers in such dark and dragging ways as those which the Fontaines explored – the ways of crime, not taken as detectives or allies of the law, but studied as scientists, with the end always in view of throwing light on causes rather

1

than on actual deeds. The next generation – it was to save this by greater knowledge that Dr. Fontaine laboured, assisted by Solange, and here at least they could hope to continue their new book on the detection of poisons undisturbed by those sudden irruptions of the actual, such as the affair of the negro girl at Marseilles, which so violently tore the tissues of their ordered life.

'Besides,' as Solange said, 'Terence and Raymond will be able to come up from Nice and see us, and that will be ever so much nicer than always being alone.'

Her father glanced at her sharply, to see whether there were any change of her quiet, clear pallor, but eye and cheek were as calm as ever. Terence Corkery – the Consul from Nice – he was an old friend, and as such Solange was wont to treat him, in that affectionate yet aloof way of hers, but young Raymond Ker, with the alertness of a newer civilisation in his confident jaw and bright eyes – he was a comparatively new acquaintance, and though it was true he had been with Solange through much – the tragic affair of the 'Green Parrakeet', and the more grotesque happening at the draper's shop in Marseilles – yet it was unlike Solange to admit any man to quite that degree of intimacy so swiftly. Therefore, Dr. Fontaine had wondered, but the clear oval of his daughter's face gave him no clue. He resigned himself to the fact that he could read the countenance of a homicidal maniac with greater ease and accuracy than the familiar features of his daughter.

Corkery was unable to leave Nice while the Fontaines were at St. Lys that year, but, true to his promise, Raymond, protesting that he was merely on the look-out for 'copy', arrived at the grey town in the mountains one heavenly evening in June. Solange objected.

'How can you expect copy here, Raymond? This is the abode of innocence and peace. Nothing ever happens, except births and deaths, and the few there are of the latter are invariably from old age!'

'You forget you are a stormy petrel, Solange,' replied Raymond, only half-jesting. 'I always have hopes of something happening where you are.'

But as Solange looked annoyed, and he remembered her distaste for crime encountered in individuals, he changed the conversation. And just at first it looked as though Raymond were out in his theory, and as though peace must always be absolute at St. Lys. Never was there a place that seemed so as though the *bon Dieu* kept it in His pocket, as the Fontaines' old servant, Marie, expressed it. There were not many people to know, socially speaking, and the only family with whom the Fontaines visited on at all a society footing – though both Solange and her father cared little for that sort of thing and made friends with every butcher and baker – was that of the De Tourvilles. M. De Tourville was the lord of the manor, a moth-eaten old castle, beautiful from sheer age and fitness for its surroundings, picturesque enough to set all Raymond's American enthusiasms alight, but shabby to an extent that made Madame De Tourville's conversation one perpetual wail. She was a thin, feverish-looking woman, not without a burnt-out air of handsomeness in her straight features and large eyes, but looking older than her husband, though she was a year or so the younger. He was a very picturesque figure, as he went about the windy town in the long blue cloak he affected, his head, where the dark hair was only beginning to be faintly silvered, bare, and his thin, hawk-like face held high. A queer man, perhaps, said the townspeople, with his sudden tempers, his deep angers, his impulsive kindnesses, but a man of whom they were all proud. They felt the beauty of his presence in the town, though they could not have expressed it. Madame they liked less; she came from the hard Norman country, and was reported to be more than a little miserly, more so than was necessary even on the meagre income of the De Tourville family.

It was for his sake that everyone had been glad, and not a little curious, when a very rich lady, a young lady, who was a cousin and ward of the De Tourvilles, had come to live with them at the castle. That money should come into the old place, even if only temporarily, was felt to be right, and deep in the minds of the women was the unspoken wonder as to how thin, feverish madame would fare with a young girl in the household. For though he was forty-five, M. De Tourville had the romantic air which, to some young girls, is more attractive than youth.

So much detail about the De Tourvilles was common gossip, and had filtered from the notary's wife, viâ the hotel-keeper's wife, to Marie, and thence to Solange. She herself had visited the château several times, for mutual friends in Paris had supplied letters of introduction, and she knew enough of the De Tourville household to have interested Raymond in them before she and her father took him to call at the château.

Raymond was of opinion that Solange had not exaggerated in depicting the household as interesting. There was something about the bleak château, with its faded tapestries and ill-kept terraces, which would have

5

stirred romance in the dullest, but when added to it was a family that to nerves at all sensitive gave a curious impression of under-currents, then interest was bound to follow. Several times during that call Raymond wondered whether Solange had got her 'feeling' about this household, whether that was what interested her, or whether for once he were being more sensitive, perhaps unduly so. For Solange talked gaily, seemed her usual self.

The De Tourville couple were as she had pictured them. The chief interest lay in the personality of Mademoiselle Monique Levasseur, the young ward. She was not, strictly speaking, pretty, but she had a force born of her intense vitality, her evident joy in life. Her dark eyes, large and soft, with none of the beadiness of most brown eyes, glowed in the healthy pallor of her face, her rather large, mobile mouth was deeply red, and her whole girlish form – too thin, with that exquisite appealing meagreness which means extreme youth – seemed vibrant with life. Yet she had her softnesses too – for her cousin, Edmund De Tourville. Her schoolgirl worship was evident in the direction of her limpid gaze, her childish eagerness to wait on him, which he was too much *galant homme* to allow. How much of it all did the wife see,

6

wondered Raymond? He watched the quiet, repressed woman as she dispensed tea, and could gather little from her impassivity. Once he caught a gleam, not between man and girl, but between man and wife – a gleam that surely spoke of the intimacy that needs no words – and felt oddly reassured. The couple understood each other, probably smiled, not heartlessly, tenderly even, with the benignant pity of knowledge, at the schoolgirl enthusiasm. Doubtless that was the under-current that he had felt in the relations between the three. Yet, only a few minutes later, he doubted whether that impression were the true one. For, as they were about to leave, M. De Tourville spoke a few words low to the girl, and she got up and left the room, to reappear a moment later with a little tray, on which was a medicine-bottle and a glass. Everyone looked as they felt, a little surprised, and Edmund De Tourville, measuring out a dose of the medicine carefully, said, smiling:

'You must pardon these domesticities, but the wife has not been well for some time, and the doctor lays great stress on the importance of her taking her drops regularly. Is it not so, Thérèse?'

And Madame De Tourville, obediently draining the little glass, replied that it was. Nothing much in that little incident, but as the girl bore the tray away again her guardian opened the door for her, and slipped out after her; and Raymond, who was by the door, was made the unwilling, but inevitably curious, spectator of an odd little scene. The door did not quite close, and swung a little way open again after De Tourville had pulled it after him, and Raymond saw the girl put the tray down on the buffet which stood in the passage, saw De Tourville catch her as she turned to come back, and saw the hurried kiss that he pressed on her upturned brow. It was not at all a passionate kiss, though. But the girl glowed beneath it like the rose, and Raymond, with a sudden compunction, moved across the room, so that he was away from the door when his host came in. He was not surprised that Monique Levasseur did not return.

That evening Raymond said to Solange, as they were smoking their after-dinner cigarettes in the hotel garden, which hung on the mountain side, the one word:

'Well?'

And Solange, looking up at him, laughed.

'Well? You mean about this afternoon? You're getting very elliptic, my friend.'

'One can, with you.'

'And – "well" meant do I think there is anything – anything odd?'

He nodded.

'Yes,' said Solange. 'I do. But I can't for the life of me say what.'

'The girl is obviously in love with him.'

'Oh, that – yes. That doesn't matter. She is of the age. But a schoolgirl's rave on a man much older than herself wouldn't make me feel there was anything odd, not if he were married ten deep. No, it was something – something more sinister than that.'

'What do you make of the girl?' asked Raymond.

'A personality, evidently. But of the passive kind.'

'Passive?' ejaculated Raymond, in surprise; 'she struck me as being most amazingly vital, and vital people aren't passive.'

'Vital women can be. For the height of femininity is an acutely enhanced passivity. The women who made history, the Helens and Cleopatras, didn't go out and do things, they just lay about and things happened. In the annals of crime, also, you will find frequently that women who are as wax have not only inspired crimes, but helped to commit them, or even committed them alone, acting under the orders of their lovers, as Jeanne Weiss did when she tried to poison her husband. It is a definite type. There are, of course, women who are the dominating force, such as Lady Macbeth; but the other kind is quite as forceful in its effects.'

'You are not suggesting, I suppose, that little Monique Levasseur –'

'No, indeed. I got nothing but what was sweet and rather pathetic and feminine with her. But the fact remains that passionate passivity may turn to anything.'

And Solange drifted off to discussion of actual cases, such as those of the two sinister Gabrielles – she who was wife of Fenayrou, and she who was accomplice of Eyraud, and from them to that most pathetic of all the examples of feminine docility, Mary Blandy, who poisoned her father for the sake of her lover. And after that, secret poisoning, that abominable and most enthralling of all forms of murder, held them talking about its manifestations till Dr. Fontaine came out to smoke a last pipe.

A month flew past in that enchanted city of towers, and though the Fontaines met the family from the château now and then, no greater degree of intimacy was arrived at between them; indeed, since the arrival of Raymond, the De Tourvilles seemed to withdraw themselves and Monique much more than they had before. Then one day, M. De Tourville arrived at the hotel, only a day before the Fontaines were leaving it, with a request that only intimacy or a great necessity justified. He soon proved that he had the latter to urge him. He told them that his wife, who had been ailing for a long time, as they were aware, had been ordered away, and had left the day before for Switzerland, for a sanatorium, and he asked them whether they would be so good as to take charge of Mademoiselle Levasseur, and escort her to Paris to the house of her former *gouvernante,* at whose school she had been before coming to St. Lys? He could not as a man alone – despite his grey hairs, he added with a smile – continue to look after Monique. But if Monsieur and Mademoiselle Fontaine would accord him this favour, he could himself come to Paris later, and make sure that all was well with his ward. What he said was very reasonable, and Solange and her father agreed willingly.

But Raymond saw the long look that the girl turned on her guardian from the window of the train as they were starting, saw the meaning glance with which he replied, and somehow that little scene in the passage flashed up against his memory, clear and vivid. Solange said nothing much, but she was kindness itself to the girl, who was plainly depressed at leaving the god of her adoration, and not till the Fontaines had themselves

11

arrived in Switzerland, whither they were bound – a fact she had not thought needful to mention to M. De Tourville – did Solange say anything to her father. And then it was only to express a little wonder that at the place where M. De Tourville, when she had asked him, had said his wife was staying, there was no trace of any lady of that name to be found.

Raymond had gone over to New York by then, and this little discovery, which would so have interested him, he was not destined to know till the following spring. For in February of the next year – which is when spring begins in the gracious country of southern France, Solange somehow made her father feel that another little stay in St. Lys – which, as a matter of fact, had rather bored him – was just what he wanted, and there Raymond, once again on his travels, joined them for a fleeting week. It was less than a year since they had first met the De Tourvilles at St. Lys, yet in that time two things had happened which vitally altered life at the château. Madame De Tourville had died in Switzerland, without ever having returned to her home, and M. De Tourville was married to the ward who had so plainly adored him in the days gone by.

12

Solange had enjoyed those months which had elapsed between the two visits to St. Lys. Her work had been purely theoretical during the whole of that time; any problems which the continued presence of Raymond might have evoked had been in abeyance owing to his protracted absence on business for his paper, and her father's book had been a success in the only way that appealed to him and his daughter – a success among the *savants* of their particular line of work. Yet, when she heard of the new marriage of De Tourville, she went back to St. Lys, though she knew it meant for her work of the kind she liked least.

When Raymond heard of the changes at the château his mouth and eyes fell open, and he stared at Solange, marvelling that she could tell him so tranquilly. True, she had not seen what he had, that furtive kiss, but yet, where was her gift, what had happened to her famous power of feeling evil, of being aware of dangers to society in her fellow-men, dangers even only contemplated? She had told him calmly, in answer to his questions, that the death of Madame De Tourville seemed certainly mysterious. She had never returned to the home from which she had been so secretively hurried away, no one but her husband, who had joined her in Switzerland, had seen her die – that is to say, no one who knew her in the little world of St. Lys, and as for anyone else, they had only her husband's word to take. She had simply ceased to be, as quietly and unobtrusively as she had lived, and the graceful, passionate young girl, who, however unconsciously, had been her rival, had taken her place.

Yet, or so thought Raymond, when first he met him on this second visit, De Tourville did not look a happy man. There was a haunted expression in his deep-set eyes, a queer watchfulness about his manner, a brooding there had never been before about his eagle face. Perhaps, as Solange suggested, this was because his young bride – as adoring and far more charming than before, as the new-opened rose surpasses the tightly folded bud – was ailing in health. The air of the mountains seemed too keen for her, or the fates envied her her transparent happiness – no cloud upon that! If she, too, were involved in that which Raymond could hardly bear even in his thoughts to bring against the man, then was she the most perfect example of the man-moulded woman of whom Solange had spoken, who had ever existed.

There were days on which she seemed almost her old self, though her husband always watched to see she did not tire herself, but again there were other days, increasing in number, when it seemed that she lost strength with every breath she drew, and then nothing but her husband's ministrations would satisfy her, no hand but his was allowed so much as to alter her cushions or give her a glass of water. And, watching the man as he waited on her, and detecting that haunted something in his face, Raymond thought what a bitter irony it was, if indeed he had unlawfully hurried his wife out of this world, that now this more dearly loved woman for whom he had sinned should also be drawing nearer to the brink, and, most poignant irony of all, if his hand had indeed given, in the much-paraded medicine, poison to his first wife, how every time the second refused to accept anything save at that same hand it must seem to him, in his conscience-ridden mind, as though nothing which his hand poured out could bring anything but death.

Yet all that was sheer trickery of the mind, and a man strong enough to carry through a crime would perhaps be beyond such promptings of the nerves? But De Tourville did not seem so immune, Raymond thought, and Solange was forced to agree with him. She, too, was beginning to look worried, to his practised eyes, and he could not but feel a shade of triumph. What if it were he, after all, who had detected what those acute senses of

15

hers had passed over? Yet when he examined himself, Raymond was not sure what he wanted. If De Tourville had indeed hurried his wife away – as he had undeniably hurried with indecent haste into his second marriage – did he still want him to be found out and tried for the crime? What then of the fragile Monique, with her big eyes where happiness fought with physical discomfort, and won every time they rested on her husband? A murderer was a dreadful thing, a secret poisoner the basest of murderers, yet what had the first Madame De Tourville to recommend her, to put it with brutal frankness? Nothing compared with this ardent, gracious girl. And, as though the gods themselves were of Raymond's mind, Monique De Tourville's health began to mend, and with that mending the shadow seemed to pass from the face of her husband. He seemed as a man who has taken a new lease of life, as though in his veins also the blood flowed more strongly, and in his heart resurgent life beat higher. On one thing he was determined – to remove his young wife from the place that had seemed to agree with her so ill. Never again, so he declared, should her life be risked in the château, even though it had been in his family for a thousand years, and, to the horror of the town, the historical

16

old place was put up for sale, and bought by an American millionaire. Raymond's good offices were called in over the deal; indeed it was he, triumphing over scruples, who had first led the wealthy personage down to St. Lys to see the castle. The sale had been concluded, all was ready for the departure of Monique and her husband for South America – a climate M. De Tourville had persuaded himself was just what she needed – when the most terrible yet most thrilling day St. Lys had ever known was upon it.

Solange had announced that she was going up to the château to see if she could help the still delicate Monique with her final arrangements – the De Tourvilles were leaving in an automobile to catch the Paris express at midday. Solange had seemed to Raymond's observant eyes oddly watchful of late; he marked well-known symptoms in her, but could not fathom their cause.

Did she, like himself, suspect the picturesque Edmund De Tourville, and even if so, had she, after her individualistic fashion, which often made her take the law into her own hands when she judged fit, decided that Monique's happiness was the important thing, and that Edmund must be allowed to go free for the sake of the girl who hung upon him? It would not be unlike Solange.

If, according to her classification of criminals into the congenital and the occasional, De Tourville merely came into the latter, and had only committed the one crime that almost any of us may, if hard enough pressed, and would be safe never to commit another, then it was more than possible she would think he should be allowed to work out his own salvation. If, on the other hand, she had cause to consider him one of those born killers to whom their own desires are sufficient warrant to prey upon society, then, he knew, she would not sacrifice the community to one girl – even apart from the fact that the girl herself might be the next victim. Human tigers, such as are the born killers, are creatures who tired quickly, and who had violent reactions.

Or was he, Raymond, perhaps conjuring up out of a few unfortunately suspicious circumstances a crime that had never been committed, and had the death of Thérèse De Tourville, after all, been merely a convenient but purely natural happening? But against that hope was his knowledge that Solange was aware of something odd in the *affaire* De Tourville, though she had never admitted so much to him.

He walked by her side up to the château on this May morning with a strange quickening of the heart. There seemed a hush as of

18

expectation in the crisp, still air; on the quiet lips of Solange; above all, in the watchful look of De Tourville, whose eyes bore the look of one who is calculating time as though every minute were precious.

Monique alone was radiant, stronger than she had been for some time past, fired with excitement at the thought of the new life in the new world. Raymond had long persuaded himself that, whatever sinister meaning lay behind the drama of the château, she had had no hand in it. Wax as she was in her husband's hands, Raymond told himself her glance was too frank and clear for a guilt to lie behind those eyes.

The big *salon* at the château was dismantled, the pictures were gone from the walls, and packing-cases, already labelled, stood about the bare floor. Edmund had had to sell his family place, but he was taking the most loved of his possessions with him.

'*Cherie*, how sweet of you to come!' cried Monique, springing up from the crate on which she was sitting, already attired in her little close-fitting motor-bonnet that framed her face like a nun's coif, the soft, white chiffon veil streaming behind her, only her full, passionate lips giving the lie to the conventual aspect of her. She kissed Solange, then held out both hands eagerly to Raymond.

'Oh, I'm so excited! And I believe Edmund is, too, though he pretends he isn't. I think he is afraid of something happening to prevent us going!'

'What should happen?' asked Edmund, more harshly than was his wont in addressing her.

'Exactly! That's what I say. What should or could? But I do feel you're anxious all the same, Edmund.'

And Monique nodded with an air of womanly wisdom that was new to her.

At that moment a knocking was heard at the great door – an old wooden structure with a heavy iron knocker. The rapping was insistent, even violent, and to each person there came the sudden feeling that something beyond the usual stood there and made that urgent summons. Of all the people there none seemed so disturbed as Edmund De Tourville. His dark face became very pale, but he did not move.

They heard old Henri, the butler, shuffle to the door, and the next moment came the sound of confused protests, asseverations, then over all rose a voice they knew, but which seemed to two of the people in the *salon* to be a voice out of a dream.

Quick, sharp footsteps came near, the door was flung wide open, and Thérèse De

Tourville stood upon the threshold, her head flung back, her eyes blazing in her white face, surveying them all as they stared at her. Then Solange moved swiftly forward to Monique's side, as though to protect her. The girl had fallen back and was staring at this ghost from the dead year, and Raymond's face was like hers. Only De Tourville and Solange did not look amazed; for his part he seemed as a man stricken by a blow he has long dreaded.

'Thérèse – Thérèse,' the unfortunate man stammered, 'have you no pity?'

'Pity!' said Madame De Tourville – the only Madame De Tourville – in a harsh voice. 'No, I do not pity. I leave that to you, who cannot even carry out what you begin, who weaken in everything. Pity!'

Raymond interposed. He never knew – did not dare ask himself – whether his first feeling had not been regret that Thérèse De Tourville still lived, that her husband had not, as she taunted him, finished what he had begun; but he did know that the immediate thing was to try and shield Monique from greater pain than she must inevitably be made to feel.

'There can be no need for Madame De – for Monique to be here,' he said. 'Solange, take her away.'

'Yes,' said De Tourville, with a groan, 'take her away quickly!'

21

'Not till she has heard!' cried Thérèse; and planted her tall, thin form against the door.

Behind her the frightened faces of the servants could be seen peering.

Then De Tourville broke down.

'Thérèse, I beg of you – anything but that! I will give you anything you like – the money, all of it; we both will! But do not say anything, I implore you! Thérèse –'

Then Monique astonished them all. She gently shook off Solange's detaining hand and went and stood by Edmund, looking at the other woman fiercely.

'Go on!' she said. 'What have you to say that can hurt me? You are here, and I am not his wife! What can anything else matter?'

'You don't understand,' said Raymond urgently. 'Come away.'

'What don't I understand?'

'Your Edmund,' began Madame De Tourville, 'is not only a bigamist! He is a murderer, an assassin, or would be if he had had the heart to finish what he began! What do you say to that, you white-faced bit of sentiment?'

'Edmund, it isn't true?' stammered Monique, her eyes fixed on him.

He could only bow his head in reply; all the fight seemed to have gone out of him.

Again Monique surprised them. She flung

22

her arms round Edmund and held him fiercely.

'Edmund – and you were willing to do that for me?'

Wonder, sorrow, and – yes – triumph rang in her voice. In that moment Raymond Ker learnt more about women than in the whole of his thirty years previously.

'Take her away quickly, before she learns the truth!' said Solange urgently to Edmund above the girl's head.

His eyes met hers with desperation in their haggard depths. He swung Monique's frail figure up in his arms and made to carry her from the room, but Thérèse only laughed and still barred the way.

'For you!' she said. 'For you! You little fool! Did you think he had tried to poison *me?* It was all arranged between us! I was to disappear and be given out for dead, and he was to marry you and kill you for the money! It is you he has been poisoning, not me!'

And she laughed again.

'It isn't possible!' cried Raymond. 'De Tourville, why don't you say something? Don't you see it's killing Monique?'

'Tell her – I can't!' muttered De Tourville to Solange.

Monique had dropped her hands from him and had taken a step back; in her white, stricken face her eyes looked suddenly dim, like those of a dying bird. Solange took her gently by the arm.

'Monique, it's true,' she said. 'I'm afraid you've got to know it's true. But he repented, Monique; he hadn't the heart to go on with it. He grew to love you too dearly. Monique –'

'What does all that matter!' said Monique. 'He tried to kill me – to kill me! Oh, it's a joke! You're making it up, all of you! Say it's a joke, say it isn't true! Say it – say it!'

No one stirred; and her voice, which had sharpened to the wild scream of a child, fell into monotony again.

'So it's true? All that time I was ill – that I was so thirsty, that my throat hurt so, and I was so sick – you were doing it, Edmund? When no one but you looked after me, you were doing it all the time?'

'Not all the time. He could not go on with it,' said Solange. 'You remember when you began to get better? That was when he found he cared for you too much.'

'It doesn't matter,' repeated Monique.

'Well, it's brought me back, anyway,' said Madame De Tourville coarsely. 'I wasn't going to be cheated because a weak fool had succumbed to your pretty face and soft ways. Where did I come in, I should like to know? At first when I wrote and said what a

24

long time it was taking, he always replied that he had to go cautiously, that Dr. Fontaine and this so-clever *demoiselle* were here, and would suspect if anything happened too soon. And I went on believing him. Then I got suspicious. I kept on picturing them together – my husband and this girl he ought to have killed long ago – and I knew if he wasn't killing her he must be kissing her. So I made inquiries, and found out they were going to do a flit, with the money that should have been mine by now, mine and his. And here I am.'

She finished her extraordinary speech, with its astounding egotism, its brutal claims on what could not conceivably be considered hers, and folded her strong arms across her meagre chest, shooting out her hard jaw contemptuously. There could be little doubt which was the stronger willed of the two – she or her husband.

'The question is,' remarked Solange, in what she purposely made a very matter-of-fact tone, 'what is going to be done about it all now? I suppose everyone in the town saw you come here, madame?'

'Certainly. I am sick of hiding myself.'

'You do not mind going to prison with your husband, then?'

'I care for nothing except to get him from that girl. The money is lost, of course. Well

25

and good, but at least he shan't have the girl, either.'

Solange turned to Monique.

'Monique, it rests with you,' she said gently. 'Are you going to prosecute? To give information against these people? They trapped you into a marriage that was a sham, because it was their only way of making sure of the money, and then they tried to kill you. Are you going to let them go free?'

Monique had followed the speech carefully, her lips sometimes moving soundlessly as though she were repeating the words that Solange used to herself the better to impress them upon her dazed brain. Slowly she turned her eyes, as with a strong effort of will, from the face of Solange to that of Edmund De Tourville. He had not spoken since his outburst to Solange, but he had not taken his eyes from Monique. Now he made no appeal, he only moistened his lips with his tongue and waited.

'I won't hurt you,' said Monique slowly.

'Oh, the hussy, the wretch!' cried Madame De Tourville. 'She is not going to prosecute because she still wants him. She couldn't be with him if he went to prison, and she still wants him. Shameful hussy, that's what I call you!'

And the odd thing was that Madame De

Tourville was perfectly genuine in her indignation.

'Monique, I can't thank you,' said De Tourville slowly. 'Thanks from me to you would be an insult. I can only tell you –'

'Ah, la la, they will pay each other compliments in a minute!' broke in Madame De Tourville. 'It's as well I made up my mind to what I did before I came here.'

'What do you mean?' asked Monique quickly.

'I mean that I called in on monsieur the magistrate on my way, and he and his gendarmes are waiting at the door now for me and my husband. Oh, I wasn't going to run the risk of your forgiving him!'

And Thérèse turned, walked across the hall, where the pale-faced servants fell back from her in fear, and opened the door to the police.

'Well,' said Raymond to Solange late that evening – 'well, what do you know about that? They'll get twenty years with hard labour if they get a day, and that woman gave the whole thing away deliberately when she could have got off scot free. Monique would never have brought the charge. It's jolly hard on her, the whole story'll have to come out now.'

'Exactly,' said Solange, 'that's why Thérèse has done it. That woman has two passions – money and her husband. She thought the former was the stronger when she planned to let him marry the girl as a preliminary to poisoning her, and so it might have been if De Tourville had not played her false. Then she could keep quiet no longer, and she thinks a lifetime in prison cheap so long as she is avenged on him. It is all a question of values. After all, murder is the action behind which lies more distortion of value than behind any other in the world, so you must not be surprised that, when you have found someone who can think it worth while to murder, they are abnormal in their other values also.'

'Perhaps not – but it isn't only Madame De Tourville who needs explaining. What of him? A weak man who repented, who couldn't be true even to an infamous contract?'

'More or less, though in a man of his type there would always be a thousand complications and subtleties that make any sweeping statement rather crude. He is a potential criminal, but in happier circumstances no one – including himself – would have ever found it out. If he could have made his get-away, I don't believe he would ever have done a criminal act again. In time he would

28

doubtless have persuaded himself that the whole thing was a nightmare, and had never taken place; have believed that he had always been devoted to Monique, and that his only sin was a bigamous marriage, which his great love almost excused. If Thérèse had never turned up to trouble them, he would probably have forgotten even that.'

'And Monique?'

'Ah, she is a true type of the *femme aux hommes*. She only lives and breathes in the loved man. You see, even as a young girl fresh from school she started an affair with Edmund, the wife did not exist for her in the strength of her passion, and it was that passion, so innocently undisguised, that first put the whole foul scheme into their heads. For you turned up, a young, eligible man, and they got panicky as they realised that she had only to marry for them to lose her money. If it were not you, it was only a question of time before it was someone else.'

'Solange, when did you guess? Did you not at one time think as I did, that De Tourville had got rid of his wife by foul means so as to marry Monique?'

'I certainly should have thought so if I had gone on the facts alone, but I went on two other things as well – my knowledge of types and my "feeling".

'I got my "feeling" about that household. I couldn't hide it from you, who knew me, and the person I got it with most was Thérèse. That he was of the type to fit in with her I knew – she is of the race of strong women, of the Mrs. Mannings and the Brinvilliers of the criminal world; he is one of the Macbeths. But the odd thing is this – if it had been he who was of the dominating criminal type instead of his wife, then he and Monique would have in all probability done as you suspected. She is no criminal as things are, but she is so completely the type of waxen woman that it would only have rested with the man to make her another Marie Vitalis or Jeanne Weiss. At first I thought as you did, and when I did not find Madame De Tourville in Switzerland, I thought it all the more, though I still couldn't fit it in with their characters as I thought they were. Then I heard of the marriage with Monique and I came back here determined to find out what was wrong. Monique's failing health struck me as very suspicious, and gradually from one little thing and another I put the crime together.'

'What would you have done if Monique had gone on being ill? Given him away, or gone to him privately?' asked Raymond.

'The former, I think, always depending on

what Monique wished. For if he could have gone on with it, it would have meant he was impossible to save. But I had hardly got all my facts, hardly tabulated her symptoms and watched them together, when his heart began to fail him, or to prompt him, whichever way you like to put it. I shall always be glad that it was so before I told him that I knew.'

'Then you did?'

'Yes, I should have told him earlier, of course, if I had seen no signs of relenting on his part, but I held out to the last minute, even at the cost of a little more physical suffering for poor little Monique, so as to give him the chance of saving his own soul alive. I knew that if ever it did come out, the knowledge that he had done so would be the only thing to save them both from madness.'

'And in his new intention – taking her away – you would have helped – you did help – knowing she was not his wife?'

'My dear, who was hurt by it?' said Solange. 'When you have seen as many people hurt as I have, that will be your chief consideration, too. I have told you young Monique is a *grande amoureuse*. Her life is bound up in him, and that was what I was out to save not merely from his poison, but from the poison of his wife's tongue. They would have

31

lived very happily in South America, both have been virtuous, and the chief criminal – his wife – would have had the severest punishment possible in the loss of husband and money. As it is, Monique may die of her hurt.'

'Actually die of a broken heart? And in the twentieth century?'

'She may indeed, for she is not a twentieth century type – she is eternal. At present she is very ill of it with papa and a hospital nurse in attendance, as you know. There is only one hope for her which may materialise, as she has at least the balm of knowing that Edmund relented of his own free will.'

'And what's that?'

'That her need of love is greater than her need of any one particular lover. That sometimes happens, you know.'

'She'll never love again,' asserted Raymond with conviction.

'I shall be more surprised if she can live without,' said Solange.

And the conversation wandered away from Monique Levasseur, and plunged – always in theoretic fashion – into the ways of love. Here Raymond refused to follow Solange, as he did in the psychology of matters criminal, and they parted company after an hour of arguing over the route.

Raymond was certain he was far more nearly right than Solange; she was only sure she was right for herself, though very probably wrong for the rest of the world. Yet a few months later it was proved that she had been right in her hope for Monique. A romantic Englishman, who attended the trial of the De Tourvilles, and 'wrote up' Monique as the heroine, was one of the many men who proposed to her on that occasion, and he succeeded in persuading her into what was to be a very happy love-marriage.

AGATHA CHRISTIE

Jane Marple in
Tape-Measure Murder

Miss Politt took hold of the knocker and rapped politely on the cottage door. After a discreet interval she knocked again. The parcel under her left arm shifted a little as she did so, and she readjusted it. Inside the parcel was Mrs Spenlow's new green winter dress, ready for fitting. From Miss Politt's left hand dangled a bag of black silk, containing a tape-measure, a pincushion, and a large, practical pair of scissors.

Miss Politt was tall and gaunt, with a sharp nose, pursed lips, and meagre iron-grey hair. She hesitated before using the knocker for the third time. Glancing down the street, she saw a figure rapidly approaching. Miss Hartnell, jolly, weather-beaten, fifty-five, shouted out in her usual loud bass voice, 'Good afternoon, Miss Politt!'

The dressmaker answered, 'Good afternoon, Miss Hartnell.' Her voice was excessively thin and genteel in its accents.

34

She had started life as a lady's maid. 'Excuse me,' she went on, 'but do you happen to know if by any chance Mrs Spenlow isn't at home?'

'Not the least idea,' said Miss Hartnell.

'It's rather awkward, you see. I was to fit on Mrs Spenlow's new dress this afternoon. Three-thirty, she said.'

Miss Hartnell consulted her wrist watch. 'It's a little past the half-hour now.'

'Yes. I have knocked three times, but there doesn't seem to be any answer, so I was wondering if perhaps Mrs Spenlow might have gone out and forgotten. She doesn't forget appointments as a rule, and she wants the dress to wear the day after tomorrow.'

Miss Hartnell entered the gate and walked up the path to join Miss Politt outside the door of Laburnam Cottage.

'Why doesn't Gladys answer the door?' she demanded. 'Oh, no, of course, it's Thursday – Gladys's day out. I expect Mrs Spenlow has fallen asleep. I don't expect you've made enough noise with this thing.'

Seizing the knocker, she executed a deafening *rat-a-tat-tat*, and in addition thumped upon the panels of the door. She also called out in a stentorian voice, 'What ho, within there!'

There was no response.

Miss Politt murmured, 'Oh, I think Mrs

35

Spenlow must have forgotten and gone out. I'll call round some other time.' She began edging away down the path.

'Nonsense,' said Miss Hartnell firmly. 'She can't have gone out. I'd have met her. I'll just take a look through the windows and see if I can find any signs of life.'

She laughed in her usual hearty manner, to indicate that it was a joke, and applied a perfunctory glance to the nearest windowpane – perfunctory because she knew quite well that the front room was seldom used, Mr and Mrs Spenlow preferring the small back sitting-room.

Perfunctory as it was, though, it succeeded in its object. Miss Hartnell, it is true, saw no signs of life. On the contrary, she saw, through the window, Mrs Spenlow lying on the hearthrug – dead.

'Of course,' said Miss Hartnell, telling the story afterwards, 'I managed to keep my head. That Politt creature wouldn't have had the least idea of what to do. "Got to keep our heads," I said to her. "*You* stay here, and I'll go for Constable Palk." She said something about not wanting to be left, but I paid no attention at all. One has to be firm with that sort of person. I've always found they enjoy making a fuss. So I was just going off when, at that very moment,

Mr Spenlow came round the corner of the house.'

Here Miss Hartnell made a significant pause. It enabled her audience to ask breathlessly, 'Tell me, how did he look?'

Miss Hartnell would then go on, 'Frankly, *I* suspected something at once! He was *far* too calm. He didn't seem surprised in the least. And you may say what you like, it isn't natural for a man to hear that his wife is dead and display no emotion whatever.'

Everybody agreed with this statement.

The police agreed with it, too. So suspicious did they consider Mr Spenlow's detachment, that they lost no time in ascertaining how that gentleman was situated as a result of his wife's death. When they discovered that Mrs Spenlow had been the monied partner, and that her money went to her husband under a will made soon after their marriage, they were more suspicious than ever.

Miss Marple, that sweet-faced – and, some said, vinegar-tongued – elderly spinster who lived in the house next to the rectory, was interviewed very early – within half an hour of the discovery of the crime. She was approached by Police Constable Palk, importantly thumbing a notebook. 'If you don't mind, ma'am, I've a few questions to ask you.'

37

Miss Marple said, 'In connection with the murder of Mrs Spenlow?'

Palk was startled. 'May I ask, madam, how you got to know of it?'

'The fish,' said Miss Marple.

The reply was perfectly intelligible to Constable Palk. He assumed correctly that the fishmonger's boy had brought it, together with Miss Marple's evening meal.

Miss Marple continued gently. 'Lying on the floor in the sitting-room, strangled – possibly by a very narrow belt. But whatever it was, it was taken away.'

Palk's face was wrathful. 'How that young Fred gets to know everything –'

Miss Marple cut him short adroitly. She said, 'There's a pin in your tunic.'

Constable Palk looked down, startled. He said, 'They do say, "See a pin and pick it up, all the day you'll have good luck." '

'I hope that will come true. Now what is it you want me to tell you?'

Constable Palk cleared his throat, looked important, and consulted his notebook. 'Statement was made to me by Mr Arthur Spenlow, husband of the deceased. Mr Spenlow says that at two-thirty, as far as he can say, he was rung up by Miss Marple, and asked if he would come over at a quarter past three as she was anxious to consult him about

38

something. 'Now, ma'am, is that true?'

'Certainly not,' said Miss Marple.

'You did not ring up Mr Spenlow at two-thirty?'

'Neither at two-thirty nor any other time.'

'Ah,' said Constable Palk, and sucked his moustache with a good deal of satisfaction.

'What else did Mr Spenlow say?'

'Mr Spenlow's statement was that he came over here as requested, leaving his own house at ten minutes past three; that on arrival here he was informed by the maid-servant that Miss Marple was "not at 'ome".'

'That part of it is true,' said Miss Marple. 'He did come here, but I was at a meeting at the Women's Institute.'

'Ah,' said Constable Palk again.

Miss Marple exclaimed, 'Do tell me, Constable, do you suspect Mr Spenlow?'

'It's not for me to say at this stage, but it looks to me as though somebody, naming no names, had been trying to be artful.'

Miss Marple said thoughtfully, 'Mr Spenlow?'

She liked Mr Spenlow. He was a small, spare man, stiff and conventional in speech, the acme of respectability. It seemed odd that he should have come to live in the country, he had so clearly lived in towns all his life. To Miss Marple he confided the

39

reason. He said, 'I have always intended, ever since I was a small boy, to live in the country some day and have a garden of my own. I have always been very much attached to flowers. My wife, you know, kept a flower shop. That's where I saw her first.'

A dry statement, but it opened up a vista of romance. A younger, prettier Mrs Spenlow, seen against a background of flowers.

Mr Spenlow, however, really knew nothing about flowers. He had no idea of seeds, of cuttings, of bedding out, of annuals or perennials. He had only a vision – a vision of a small cottage garden thickly planted with sweet-smelling, brightly coloured blossoms. He had asked, almost pathetically, for instruction, and had noted down Miss Marple's replies to questions in a little book.

He was a man of quiet method. It was, perhaps, because of this trait, that the police were interested in him when his wife was found murdered. With patience and perseverence they learned a great deal about the late Mrs Spenlow – and soon all St Mary Mead knew it, too.

The late Mrs Spenlow had begun life as a between-maid in a large house. She had left that position to marry the second gardener, and with him had started a flower shop in

London. The shop had prospered. Not so the gardener, who before long had sickened and died.

His widow carried on the shop and enlarged it in an ambitious way. She had continued to prosper. Then she had sold the business at a handsome price and embarked upon matrimony for the second time – with Mr Spenlow, a middle-aged jeweller who had inherited a small and struggling business. Not long afterwards, they had sold the business and come down to St Mary Mead.

Mrs Spenlow was a well-to-do woman. The profits from her florist's establishment she had invested – 'under spirit guidance', as she explained to all and sundry. The spirits had advised her with unexpected acumen.

All her investments had prospered, some in quite a sensational fashion. Instead, however, of this increasing her belief in spiritualism, Mrs Spenlow basely deserted mediums and sittings, and made a brief but wholehearted plunge into an obscure religion with Indian affinities which was based on various forms of deep breathing. When, however, she arrived at St Mary Mead, she had relapsed into a period of orthodox Church-of-England beliefs. She was a good deal at the vicarage, and attended church services with assiduity. She patronized the village shops, took an interest in the local happenings, and played village bridge.

A humdrum, everyday life. And – suddenly – murder.

Colonel Melchett, the chief constable, had summoned Inspector Slack.

Slack was a positive type of man. When he had made up his mind, he was sure. He was quite sure now. 'Husband did it, sir,' he said.

'You think so?'

'Quite sure of it. You've only got to look at him. Guilty as hell. Never showed a sign of grief or emotion. He came back to the house knowing she was dead.'

'Wouldn't he at least have tried to act the part of the distracted husband?'

'Not him, sir. Too pleased with himself. Some gentlemen can't act. Too stiff.'

'Any other woman in his life?' Colonel Melchett asked.

'Haven't been able to find any trace of one. Of course, he's the artful kind. He'd cover his tracks. As I see it, he was just fed up with his wife. She'd got the money, and I should say was a trying woman to live with – always taking up with some 'ism' or other. He cold-bloodedly decided to do away with her and live comfortably on his own.'

'Yes, that could be the case, I suppose.'

'Depend upon it, that was it. Made his plans careful. Pretended to get a phone call –'

Melchett interrupted him. 'No call been traced?'

'No, sir. That means either that he lied, or that the call was put through from a public telephone booth. The only two public phones in the village are at the station and the post office. Post office it certainly wasn't. Mrs Blade sees everyone who comes in. Station it might be. Train arrives at two twenty-seven and there's a bit of a bustle then. But the main thing is *he* says it was Miss Marple who called him up, and that certainly isn't true. The call didn't come from her house, and she herself was away at the Institute.'

'You're not overlooking the possibility that the husband was deliberately got out of the way – by someone who wanted to murder Mrs Spenlow?'

'You're thinking of young Ted Gerard, aren't you, sir? I've been working on him – what we're up against there is lack of motive. He doesn't stand to gain anything.'

'He's an undesirable character, though. Quite a pretty little spot of embezzlement to his credit.'

'I'm not saying he isn't a wrong 'un. Still, he did go to his boss and own up to that

43

embezzlement. And his employers weren't wise to it.'

'An Oxford Grouper,' said Melchett.

'Yes, sir. Became a convert and went off to do the straight thing and own up to having pinched money. I'm not saying, mind you, that it mayn't have been astuteness. He may have thought he was suspected and decided to gamble on honest repentance.'

'You have a sceptical mind, Slack,' said Colonel Melchett. 'By the way, have you talked to Miss Marple at all?'

'What's *she* got to do with it, sir?'

'Oh, nothing. But she hears things, you know. Why don't you go and have a chat with her? She's a very sharp old lady.'

Slack changed the subject. 'One thing I've been meaning to ask you, sir. That domestic-service job where the deceased started her career – Sir Robert Abercrombie's place. That's where that jewel robbery was – emeralds – worth a packet. Never got them. I've been looking it up – must have happened when the Spenlow woman was there, though she'd have been quite a girl at the time. Don't think she was mixed up in it, do you, sir? Spenlow, you know, was one of those little tuppenny-ha'penny jewellers – just the chap for a fence.'

Melchett shook his head. 'Don't think

there's anything in that. She didn't even know Spenlow at the time. I remember the case. Opinion in police circles was that a son of the house was mixed up in it – Jim Abercrombie – awful young waster. Had a pile of debts, and just after the robbery they were all paid off – some rich woman, so they said, but I don't know. Old Abercrombie hedged a bit about the case – tried to call the police off.'

'It was just an idea, sir,' said Slack.

Miss Marple received Inspector Slack with gratification, especially when she heard that he had been sent by Colonel Melchett.

'Now, really, that is very kind of Colonel Melchett. I didn't know he remembered me.'

'He remembers you, all right. Told me that what you didn't know of what goes on in St Mary Mead isn't worth knowing.'

'Too kind of him, but really I don't know anything at all. About this murder, I mean.'

'You know what the talk about it is.'

'Oh, of course – but it wouldn't do, would it, to repeat just idle talk?'

Slack said, with an attempt at geniality, 'This isn't an official conversation, you know. It's in confidence, so to speak.'

'You mean you really want to know what people are saying? Whether there's any truth in it or not?'

'That's the idea.'

'Well, of course, there's been a great deal of talk and speculation. And there are really two distinct camps, if you understand me. To begin with, there are the people who think that the husband did it. A husband or a wife is, in a way, the natural person to suspect, don't you think so?'

'Maybe,' said the inspector cautiously.

'Such close quarters, you know. Then, so often, the money angle. I hear that it was Mrs Spenlow who had the money, and therefore Mr Spenlow does benefit by her death. In this wicked world I'm afraid the most uncharitable assumptions are often justified.'

'He comes into a tidy sum, all right.'

'Just so. It would seem quite plausible, wouldn't it, for him to strangle her, leave the house by the back, come across the fields to my house, ask for me and pretend he'd had a telephone call from me, then go back and find his wife murdered in his absence – hoping, of course, that the crime would be put down to some tramp or burglar.'

The inspector nodded. 'What with the money angle – and if they'd been on bad terms lately –'

But Miss Marple interrupted him. 'Oh, but they hadn't.'

'You know that for a fact?'

'Everyone would know if they'd quarrelled! The maid, Gladys Brent – she'd have soon spread it round the village.'

The inspector said feebly, 'She mightn't have known –' and received a pitying smile in reply.

Miss Marple went on. 'And then there's the other school of thought. Ted Gerard. A good-looking young man. I'm afraid, you know, that good looks are inclined to influence one more than they should. Our last curate but one – quite a magical effect! All the girls came to church – evening service as well as morning. And many older women became unusually active in parish work – and the slippers and scarfs that were made for him! Quite embarrassing for the poor young man.

'But let me see, where was I? Oh, yes, this young man, Ted Gerard. Of course, there has been talk about him. He's come down to see her so often. Though Mrs Spenlow told me herself that he was a member of what I think they call the Oxford Group. A religious movement. They are quite sincere and very earnest, I believe, and Mrs Spenlow was impressed by it all.'

Miss Marple took a breath and went on. 'And I'm sure there was no reason to believe

47

that there was anything more in it than that, but you know what people are. Quite a lot of people are convinced that Mrs Spenlow was infatuated with the young man, and that she'd lent him quite a lot of money. And it's perfectly true that he was actually seen at the station that day. In the train – the two twenty-seven down train. But of course it would be quite easy, wouldn't it, to slip out of the other side of the train and go through the cutting and over the fence and round by the hedge and never come out of the station entrance at all. So that he need not have been seen going to the cottage. And, of course, people do think that what Mrs Spenlow was wearing was rather peculiar.'

'Peculiar?'

'A kimono. Not a dress.' Miss Marple blushed. 'That sort of thing, you know, is, perhaps, rather suggestive to some people.'

'You think it was suggestive?'

'Oh, no, *I* don't think so. I think it was perfectly natural.'

'You think it was natural?'

'Under the circumstances, yes.' Miss Marple's glance was cool and reflective.

Inspector Slack said, 'It might give us another motive for the husband. Jealousy.'

'Oh, no, Mr Spenlow would never be jealous. He's not the sort of man who notices things. If his wife had gone away and left a note on the pincushion, it would be the first he'd know of anything of that kind.'

Inspector Slack was puzzled by the intent way she was looking at him. He had an idea that all her conversation was intended to hint at something he didn't understand. She said now, with some emphasis, 'Didn't *you* find any clues, Inspector – on the spot?'

'People don't leave fingerprints and cigarette ash nowadays, Miss Marple.'

'But this, I think,' she suggested, 'was an old-fashioned crime –'

Slack said sharply, 'Now what do you mean by that?'

Miss Marple remarked slowly, 'I think, you know, that Constable Palk could help you. He was the first person on the – on the "scene of the crime", as they say.'

Mr Spenlow was sitting in a deck chair. He looked bewildered. He said, in his thin, precise voice, 'I may, of course, be imagining what occurred. My hearing is not as good as it was. But I distinctly think I heard a small boy call after me, "Yah, who's a Crippen?" It – it conveyed the impression to me that he

49

was of the opinion that I had – had killed my dear wife.'

Miss Marple, gently snipping off a dead rose head, said, 'That was the impression he meant to convey, no doubt.'

'But what could possibly have put such an idea into a child's head?'

Miss Marple coughed. 'Listening, no doubt, to the opinions of his elders.'

'You – you really mean that other people think that, also?'

'Quite half the people in St Mary Mead.'

'But – my dear lady – what can possibly have given rise to such an idea? I was sincerely attached to my wife. She did not, alas, take to living in the country as much as I had hoped she would do, but perfect agreement on every subject is an impossible idea. I assure you I feel her loss very keenly.'

'Probably. But if you will excuse my saying so, you don't sound as though you do.'

Mr Spenlow drew his meagre frame up to its full height. 'My dear lady, many years ago I read of a certain Chinese philosopher who, when his dearly loved wife was taken from him, continued calmly to beat a gong in the street – a customary Chinese pastime, I presume – exactly as usual. The people of the city were much impressed by his fortitude.'

50

'But,' said Miss Marple, 'the people of St Mary Mead react rather differently. Chinese philosophy does not appeal to them.'

'But you understand?'

Miss Marple nodded. 'My Uncle Henry,' she explained, 'was a man of unusual self-control. His motto was "Never display emotion". He, too, was very fond of flowers.'

'I was thinking,' said Mr Spenlow with something like eagerness, 'that I might, perhaps, have a pergola on the west side of the cottage. Pink roses and, perhaps, wisteria. And there is a white starry flower, whose name for the moment escapes me –'

In the tone in which she spoke to her grand-nephew, aged three, Miss Marple said, 'I have a very nice catalogue here, with pictures. Perhaps you would like to look through it – I have to go up to the village.'

Leaving Mr Spenlow sitting happily in the garden with his catalogue, Miss Marple went up to her room, hastily rolled up a dress in a piece of brown paper, and, leaving the house, walked briskly up to the post office. Miss Politt, the dressmaker, lived in rooms over the post office.

But Miss Marple did not at once go through the door and up the stairs. It was just two-thirty, and, a minute late, the Much Benham bus drew up outside the post office door. It was one of the events of the day in St Mary Mead. The postmistress hurried out with parcels, parcels connected with the shop side of her business, for the post office also dealt in sweets, cheap books, and children's toys.

For some four minutes Miss Marple was alone in the post office.

Not till the postmistress returned to her post did Miss Marple go upstairs and explain to Miss Politt that she wanted her old grey crêpe altered and made more fashionable if that were possible. Miss Politt promised to see what she could do.

The chief constable was rather astonished when Miss Marple's name was brought to him. She came in with many apologies. 'So sorry – so very sorry to disturb you. You are so busy, I know, but then you have always been so very kind, Colonel Melchett, and I felt I would rather come to you instead of to Inspector Slack. For one thing, you know, I should hate Constable Palk to get into any trouble. Strictly speaking, I suppose he shouldn't have touched anything at all.'

Colonel Melchett was slightly bewildered. He said, 'Palk? That's the St Mary Mead constable, isn't it? What has he been doing?'

52

'He picked up a pin, you know. It was in his tunic. And it occurred to me at the time that it was quite probable he had actually picked it up in Mrs Spenlow's house.'

'Quite, quite. But after all, you know, what's a pin? Matter of fact he did pick the pin up just by Mrs Spenlow's body. Came and told Slack about it yesterday – you put him up to that, I gather? Oughtn't to have touched anything, of course, but as I said, what's a pin? It was only a common pin. Sort of thing any woman might use.'

'Oh, no, Colonel Melchett, that's where you're wrong. To a man's eye, perhaps, it looked like an ordinary pin, but it wasn't. It was a special pin, a very thin pin, the kind you buy by the box, the kind used mostly by dressmakers.'

Melchett stared at her, a faint light of comprehension breaking in on him. Miss Marple nodded her head several times, eagerly.

'Yes, of course. It seems to me so obvious. She was in her kimono because she was going to try on her new dress, and she went into the front room, and Miss Politt just said something about measurements and put the tape-measure round her neck – and then all she'd have to do was to cross it and pull – quite easy, so I've heard. And then, of course, she'd go outside and pull the door to and stand there knocking as though she'd just arrived. But the pin shows she'd *already been in the house.*'

'And it was Miss Politt who telephoned to Spenlow?

'Yes. From the post office at two-thirty – just when the bus comes and the post office would be empty.'

Colonel Melchett said, 'But my dear Miss Marple, why? In heaven's name, why? You can't have a murder without a motive.'

'Well, I think, you know, Colonel Melchett, from all I've heard, that the crime dates from a long time back. It reminds me, you know, of my two cousins, Antony and Gordon. Whatever Antony did always went right for him, and with poor Gordon it was just the other way about. Race horses went lame, and stocks went down, and property depreciated. As I see it, the two women were in it together.'

'In what?'

'The robbery. Long ago. Very valuable emeralds, so I've heard. The lady's maid and the tweeny. Because one thing hasn't been explained – how, when the tweeny married the gardener, did they have enough money to set up a flower shop?'

'The answer is, it was her share of the –

the swag, I think is the right expression. Everything she did turned out well. Money made money. But the other one, the lady's maid, must have been unlucky. She came down to being just a village dressmaker. Then they met again. Quite all right at first, I expect, until Mr Ted Gerard came on the scene.

'Mrs Spenlow, you see, was already suffering from conscience, and was inclined to be emotionally religious. This young man no doubt urged her to "face up" and to "come clean" and I dare say she was strung up to do it. But Miss Politt didn't see it that way. All she saw was that she might go to prison for a robbery she had committed years ago. So she made up her mind to put a stop to it all. I'm afraid you know, that she was always rather a wicked woman. I don't believe she'd have turned a hair if that nice, stupid Mr Spenlow had been hanged.'

Colonel Melchett said slowly, 'We can – er – verify your theory – up to a point. The identity of the Politt woman with the lady's maid at the Abercrombies', but –'

Miss Marple reassured him. 'It will be all quite easy. She's the kind of woman who will break down at once when she's taxed with the truth. And then, you see, I've got her

55

tape-measure. I – er – abstracted it yesterday when I was trying on. When she misses it and thinks the police have got it, well, she's quite an ignorant woman and she'll think it will prove the case against her in some way.'

She smiled at him encouragingly. 'You'll have no trouble, I can assure you.' It was the tone in which his favourite aunt had once assured him that he could not fail to pass his entrance examination into Sandhurt.

And he had passed.

VIOLA BROTHERS SHAW

Gwynn Leith in
The Mackenzie Case

'So you had a dull trip down,' laughed Clarence Cobb, our host, after some sally by my wife about our recent fellow passengers.

Five of us were sipping *frappés* on the terrace, while Mrs. Cobb showed Erik Schroeder her tropical gardens by moonlight. The Cobbs have a beautiful home outside Havana and at their request we had brought with us three dinner guests – Dr. Whitmore, the ship's surgeon; Erik Schroeder; and Leni Dill, a pretty girl in whom Schroeder had shown some interest during the trip. None of us, except Schroeder and my wife, had anything to do with the Mackenzie case.

'So dull that a man jumped overboard the first night out of New York,' replied my wife.

'The first night out!' Clarence Cobb is a lawyer. 'That's unusual. Ordinarily they wait a little longer.'

'That's what struck me, too,' commented my wife, lightly.

57

'Are you in earnest?' demanded Leni Dill. 'You mean a man really jumped off our boat?'

'Ask the doctor,' replied Gwynn. 'I don't suppose there's any reason for keeping it secret any longer.'

Dr. Whitmore regarded my wife curiously. 'How did you know, Mrs. Keats?'

'Trust Gwynn,' chuckled Clarence Cobb. 'Don't you know she's the famous Gwynn Leith? And her husband there is Colin Keats, who Dr.-Watsons her.'

The doctor, it seems, recalled my book on the Hanaford murder. Gwynn laughed off his awe. 'I just happened to have a lucky hunch. But Mr. Schroeder is a *real* detective.'

Leni Dill almost jumped out of her chair. 'Erik Schroeder –? He told me he was a big game hunter?'

Everybody laughed. 'He's solved more crimes than any man in the country,' said Gwynn. 'But he doesn't happen to have a husband to write him up.'

'I didn't hear any mention of a suicide,' remarked Clarence Cobb.

'It was kept very quiet,' explained the ship's surgeon. 'The Captain didn't want the other passengers distressed. He was somebody utterly unknown – secretary to a wealthy man on board.'

'How do you know Mackenzie is wealthy?' inquired Gwynn.

'Well, a man who travels with a secretary –' argued the doctor.

'Oh. . . . I see. . . .' said Gwynn with that look of complete innocence which immediately made me demand:

'What makes you think he isn't?'

'Well, – for one thing, he didn't tip his steward.'

'Perhaps that was the Scotch in him,' I suggested, a little annoyed that my wife had not taken me into her confidence.

'But that first night – up in the bar – he insisted on treating everybody in sight –'

'Maybe that was the rye in him.'

'Tell us about it,' coaxed Leni Dill. Gwynn referred the question to the doctor.

'All I know is that Schmidt went overboard some time Wednesday night, and nobody knows why or how.'

'Oh, come,' protested Gwynn. 'I saw you talking earnestly to Mackenzie in the bar after dinner.'

'He was merely complaining of not feeling well and I told him there are people who become ill as soon as they get on a boat. He said his secretary must be of that type, because he had gone to bed as soon as the engines started. He had had the man out

59

on the deck for a while, but he was so ill Mackenzie had had to put him back in bed. However, Mackenzie himself had crossed a dozen times and never felt sick. So I inquired what they had eaten for lunch. And when I heard tuna fish salad, I decided they were both suffering from ptomaine poisoning and suggested having a look at the secretary.

'But he asked me not to. "He's just dropped off to sleep," he told me. "He wouldn't let me send for you. Ardent Scientist, you know. But I'm not, so if there's anything you can recommend for me –" And that's all I know except that Mackenzie was quite sick for the balance of the trip.'

'But why did Schmidt commit suicide?' insisted Leni.

'Nobody knows. Nobody had ever spoken to the man. Even Mackenzie didn't know anything about his private life. Schmidt had been in his employ only a few days.'

'Well, but how did you know he committed suicide?'

'He wasn't anywhere on the boat.'

'But how did you discover he wasn't?' persisted Leni.

'From the stewards. When Mackenzie became ill he took another room on A deck and sent down a steward for his bag, cautioning him not to disturb Mr.

60

Schmidt. The steward reported that Mr. Schmidt wasn't in the room. Later the C deck steward reported that he couldn't find him. Well, after a boat has been searched, there's only one thing to think, isn't there?'

'Except, of course, why he did it,' suggested Gwynn. 'What else did the steward on C Deck have to report?'

'He only verified what Mackenzie had said. Soon after they came on board the one man went to bed. Later the other man – that was Mackenzie – rang and asked him to carry a chair out to C deck. Together they helped the sick man out. He was very sick. When the steward had freshened up the berth, he was slumped over the railing, his head on his arms, and his face looked ghastly. The steward suggested getting me. But although the man was so sick that Mackenzie had to bend down to get his answer, he wouldn't have me.

'Some time during dinner the steward went to 361 in answer to the bell. Mackenzie met him in the companionway and told him Schmidt had dropped off to sleep. "But you might look in," he said, "in a couple of hours and see if he wants anything. I'm going up on deck. Feeling a little rocky myself." And according to the steward, he *did* look rocky.'

'I thought he did, too,' said Gwynn, 'but

61

he insisted on buying more and more drinks. When he got the color of ashes of split-pea soup, I took him out on deck and heard all about how he came from Alberta; had been in the States only for short visits; how Schmidt had told him a hard-luck story, but was evidently incompetent, having selected doubtful tuna and an inferior room, to which Mackenzie couldn't bear to return – particularly as he had given Schmidt the lower. So I suggested that he get another room.'

'I noticed you were taking quite an interest in him,' I remarked, in the immemorial manner of husbands.

'Oh,' laughed my wife, 'I'm just a child at heart and I was fascinated by his wrist watch.'

'Were you in his room the morning I couldn't find you?'

'You bet. But his passion for my company seemed to have waned.'

'Serves you right. You just went in there to snoop around. Did you find anything?'

'Two things,' replied my wife. 'A faint odor of ipecac and a mirror that swung with the boat.'

'And what did they tell the Great Mind?'

'The mirror told me that the handsome Mr. Mackenzie didn't like my visit – in fact, if I'm not reading too much into a mere look, he was fairly terrified. And the ipecac – well, it's what you give croupy babies to make them vomit, isn't it, Doctor?'

'Why, Gwynn!' exclaimed Helen Cobb from the doorway, where she had been standing with Schroeder. 'You haven't been sleuthing in competition with the Real Thing?'

Erik Schroeder looked at my wife out of shrewd blue eyes. He has white hair and the hawklike features of the Conan Doyle tradition.

Leni Dill eyed him accusingly. 'Erik! You never told me there was a suicide. And Mrs. Keats knew all about it!'

'That was because I had the luck to be in the next room to Mr. Mackenzie,' said Gwynn.

I snickered. 'I don't suppose you were the one who saw the Purser about getting him that room –?'

'Well, but I had the luck to see the Captain and the First Officer go in there and to hear the doctor tell them Mr. Mackenzie was too ill to be questioned. And considering that somebody had been inquiring after Mr. Schmidt – and the engines had been reversed – I couldn't help inferring *something*. But I daresay Mr. Schroeder knows all about it, since he went in there with the Captain.'

'I wasn't there officially,' smiled Schroeder. 'The Captain merely asked me to step in

63

while he questioned Mackenzie. And I went over Schmidt's belongings to see if we could discover his identity. But there wasn't a scrap of paper – nothing that would give a clue.'

'That wasn't what I gathered from our steward,' said Gwynn.

'What did you gather from your steward?'

'That you had found some handkerchiefs and things monogrammed *P.S.* – of fine quality, but not new – which led to the belief that Mr. Schmidt had once had money. All the other things – the newer ones – were of very inferior quality.'

'Well, that's true,' admitted Schroeder. 'I thought it might supply a motive – a man who had come down in the world and couldn't take it.'

'But on the other hand,' suggested Clarence Cobb, 'he had a job –' Schroeder shrugged. 'And don't you think it strange that he carried *nothing* to identify him?'

'As if somebody had gone through his things and removed anything that *might* –' supplemented my wife.

'Look here, Mrs. Keats,' said Schroeder, 'just what have you in mind?'

'What I bet you also had in mind, Mr. Schroeder . . . that Mr. Mackenzie murdered his secretary.'

'Gwynn!' I cried. The others looked at her

64

in various degrees of amazement. When the doctor recovered his voice he was thoroughly outraged. Mackenzie was an exceptionally charming man. Schmidt had simply gone overboard.

'But *why?*'

'Violently seasick people often contemplate suicide. The man was probably a neurotic.'

'Ardent Scientists are never neurotics,' reproved Gwynn. 'Mr. Mackenzie must have overlooked that when he talked it over with you.'

The doctor looked irritated. 'I imagine sometimes Scientists go out of their minds. Even the steward said how terribly sick he was.'

'So sick that two of them had to help him out on deck.'

Schroeder had not taken his eyes from my wife's face – troubled eyes. 'What makes you think it wasn't suicide, Mrs. Keats?'

'Just a hunch,' replied Gwynn.

Schroeder continued to look grave. 'And what else?'

'Well – there was one thing, at least, that should have been in Schmidt's bag.'

'And what was that?'

'Mrs. Eddy's book. Don't you think an ardent Scientist would have had it with him on the trip?'

65

The ghost of a smile narrowed Erik Schroeder's eyes. 'I commented on that, but the Captain seemed satisfied – and I'm on a holiday. Besides, there doesn't seem to be much motive for a man to murder his secretary.'

'You have only Mackenzie's word that Schmidt *was* his secretary –'

'He's listed that way,' protested the doctor. *'Wm R. Mackenzie and Secretary.'*

'Suppose a man had found his secretary making love to his wife,' suggested Leni.

'Hardly likely,' said Schroeder. 'Mackenzie is a handsome, engaging young man and according to the steward, Schmidt was middle-aged and plain.'

'Tell me,' asked Gwynn. 'Was Schmidt a bigger man than Mackenzie?'

'No, smaller. Why?'

'Did you happen to notice Mackenzie's wrist watch?'

'An ordinary silver watch with a leather strap. I've seen them in Canada for a pound sterling.'

'And it didn't strike you as odd –?'

'Many rich men wear cheap watches while traveling. Particularly a Scotchman might –'

'But I mean about the leather strap.'

'It was apparently much worn –'

66

'What does it mean when one eyelet is badly worn, the others not at all?'

'The worn one has been used,' volunteered Clarence.

'Well, the eyelet that fastened the strap firmly around Mackenzie's wrist wasn't the used one. It was three farther down. So it looked as though the watch had been worn for a long time by somebody with a smaller wrist than Mr. Mackenzie and had only recently been taken over by Mr. M.'

'May I use your phone?' asked Schroeder. Clarence went with him and I strained my ears, but the conversation was in Spanish.

Helen Cobb's eyes widened. 'My gracious, Gwynn, you've started something. He's speaking to the Commissioner of Police!'

'I know – he's suggesting holding Mackenzie for further questioning. They naturally asked him to stay in Havana for the routine investigation. But he hasn't stirred out of his room since we landed.'

'I suppose that's what you were discussing with the chambermaid this morning?'

'It was,' replied Gwynn, utterly unabashed. 'I was trying to figure out some excuse for calling on him. I'd like to ask him how he came to hire a secretary – without references.'

Gwynn certainly plays in luck. When we reached the Nacional, there was a message from Mackenzie asking us to call him. We stopped at his room instead. William Mackenzie could not have been over twenty-six, with a fine athletic frame and a lot of curly hair and gray-blue eyes in which there was something helplessly worried as he begged us to come in.

He told us the Commissioner had been there, wearing him down with questions about Schmidt. 'I think Schroeder put him up to it. He's darned clever, Schroeder. Of course I stuck to what I told them all along.'

'Why not, if it's true?'

'But it isn't,' said Mackenzie. I hoped he didn't see the look Gwynn shot me out of those absurdly expressive brown eyes. 'We had sailed as Mackenzie and Secretary and I didn't see why certain things should be dragged in that I was anxious to keep quiet. But this Cuban chap put the screws on me pretty hard. And I'm anxious to get away. You're the only people I know in this part of the world, and I'd like to ask your advice.'

I did not look at my wife although, in case I have not mentioned it, she is very easy to look at, with dark hair going off one ear and towards the other in a natural swirl, and clothes that always make other women look either overdressed or undergroomed.

'Last Thursday,' began Mackenzie, 'I arrived in New York with my wife. We went to the Wendham Hotel. Saturday morning, a little before ten, I went out to keep a business engagement. When I came back, my wife was not there. And she was not in the dining room, or anywhere in the hotel. I opened her closet and it was bare. The bureau was empty, too. Everything belonging to my wife had been cleaned out of the place!

'While I was trying to grasp what could have happened, there was a knock at the door. A strange man stepped into the room.

"Look here, Mr. Mackenzie," he said, "my name is Schmidt. I'm the house detective. I was next to the operator when you called down to ask about Mrs. Mackenzie." And he told me he had seen my wife drive off with her bags, but had thought it better to say nothing downstairs in case there was anything in the nature of a scandal. Because there had been a man in the cab – also with bags.

'You have to understand the relationship between my wife and myself to realize my state of mind. Three years ago I took a trip to Hollywood and met my wife, who was working in pictures. In ten days we were married. Since then we had never been separated for a day – hardly an hour. And now

69

she was gone ... with another man! I was utterly stunned and grateful for this stranger's help. Alone I would not have known where to turn.

'I hadn't the faintest notion of who this other man could be. We had been in New York only two days, and together all the time. She hadn't known until the day we left that she was coming. How could she have arranged an elopement? And up on the farm we lived a very secluded life. The few people who visited us were old friends of mine.

'Schmidt went out to make some inquiries. The more I thought, the more I was baffled. I admit I have a jealous nature and I had always been watchful. I could recall nothing – no absence – no letters – no mysterious phone calls that should have made me suspicious at the time, or that offered any clue as I paced my room, waiting for Schmidt.'

'And being a suspicious man, you hadn't asked Schmidt anything about himself?' inquired Gwynn.

'Why, no. He was the house detective – and besides I was too upset to think about him. And of course I didn't know he was going to jump off a boat and get me in a mess.'

'Of course not. I suppose he asked you for money.'

'I gave him a little for immediate expenses.

70

Later, of course, I furnished money for cables and bribes and all sorts of things – a lot of money,' he concluded ruefully.

'He came back to say that the starter recalled it was a Yellow Cab, and also the man in the cab, but not his appearance. We agreed not to mention anything to anybody, since I was eager to avoid scandal and the hotel people might resent his conduct. But he was sick of his job and eager to start off as a private investigator.

'Finally he found a driver who had been picked up by a man with a gladstone bag and stopped at the Wendham for a lady answering the description of Mrs. Mackenzie. He had driven them to the Ward Line pier. The *Orizaba* had sailed that Saturday. And Schmidt's next report was that a tall blonde in a black coat with a Persian collar and a man with a gladstone bag had sailed on the *Orizaba*.

'Schmidt offered to trail them. Of course I wanted to go, too. He made all the arrangements. I was too stunned to do more than follow his instructions. I swear to God that's all I know about Philip Schmidt. But you can see why I didn't immediately blurt it out when I was questioned.'

'Of course,' said Gwynn. 'You certainly seem to be having hard luck. And now that you're eager to be after your wife, they hold you here. Have you made any inquiries at all?'

'No. I didn't think it wise – feeling that I was under surveillance.'

'There!' said I to my wife as we were getting ready for bed. 'What do you think of your murder case now?'

'I admit I have an entirely different slant on it. Let's talk to Schroeder tomorrow. . . . But doesn't it seem funny that Schmidt, having secured the kind of job he wanted, should take himself off so mysteriously?' And she began to sing: "Just for a handful of ptomaine he left us –"

I turned out the light.

The next day we called at Schroeder's hotel. He had already seen Mackenzie who, on Gwynn's advice, had told him the story. Schroeder was surprised that Mackenzie had confided in us.

'It's because I wore my Girl Scout badge,' said Gwynn. 'Matter of fact, I don't know whether he wanted our advice half so much as our money. He was dying to get us into a game.'

'What kind of game?'

'Any kind – as soon as he heard we were bad money players.'

I am always amazed at how mean and

suspicious Gwynn can be when she doesn't like a person.

'I don't like him, either,' admitted Schroeder, 'but I've checked his story. Mackenzie and his wife registered at the Wendham from Edmonton. She left two days later. However, the starter couldn't recall whether she left alone, and denied having given any information about a Yellow Cab. In fact, Schmidt was unknown at the Wendham and they employed no house detective.

'So any deception seems to have been on the part of Schmidt. I haven't the faintest idea what his game was. But since he's gone, why bother? We have also had word from Edmonton that a William R. Mackenzie lives there, and that he left last week for New York with his wife. So there seems no further reason for holding Mackenzie and I understand the Cuban police have told him he may go.'

'May I make a suggestion?' said Gwynn. 'Before he checks out, ask him what his business was in New York, and what his wife's name is. Perhaps, if he is so anxious to trace her, he will show you a picture.'

'But why? What have you in mind?'

'Nothing,' replied Gwynn, 'only I'd like to see the type of woman who would run out on a man like Mackenzie. Of course, it may

73

have been his stinginess. But then, there was that lavish display in the bar. If a tight man loosens up to that extent, there must be some reason. The reason is missing. A lot of things are missing. Principally why Schmidt killed himself.'

The following morning Mackenzie tapped on our door to ask us whether we wouldn't care for a chukker of backgammon – which we wouldn't – and to tell us he had been released by the authorities.

'That's fine,' said Gwynn. 'I suppose you can't wait to start looking for your wife. How are you going about it?'

He gestured helplessly. 'I don't know where to begin.'

'How about the Commissioner?' I suggested.

'How about Erik Schroeder?' suggested Gwynn. 'If anybody can find her, Schroeder can.'

'But he'll want too much money. And besides, I don't like him. What concern is it of his what my business was in New York? Matter of fact, I wouldn't mind telling it to you. If you're writers, you might be able to use it. It would make a great yarn.'

My wife and I exchanged that certain look. Everybody has a story that would make a great yarn. And everybody is so generous in the manner of telling it!

'I've been working on an invention in Canada. I needn't tell you what it is – but it has to do with film. It should be worth a fortune if properly marketed. Of course it's tough dealing with those big corporations and the proper approach is as important as the invention.

'Well, one day I got a letter from a man named Paul Stone outlining a scheme for promoting my patent. And the details of the scheme were exactly as I had dreamed them. I don't know how he got wind of my invention, because I kept it very quiet. I have my own laboratory. My wife helped me and not another soul knew about it. Naturally I wrote back to Stone and he suggested that I come to New York and talk it over. He wanted me to come alone, but at the last minute I decided to take my wife. I felt she was entitled to a trip.'

'Also, wives get into trouble if they're left alone.'

'I thought of that. So she came along.'

'Eagerly, I'll bet?'

'Well, of course, she claimed she had no clothes, but – This fellow Stone had reserved a room for me at the Wendham and we went there. I found a wire saying he had been called out of town, but would be back Saturday. So my wife and I went sight-seeing and Saturday morning Stone phoned and asked me to meet him in the lobby of the Alamac.'

'Up on 71st Street?'

'That's it. Well, I waited awhile, and then had him paged, and then waited some more. Then I inquired at the desk whether he was in his room. They told me there was no Paul Stone registered at the Alamac! I didn't know what to make of it, because I had always written him there. However, he had brought me all the way from Alberta for that appointment and I was sure he meant to keep it. But at one o'clock I went back to my own hotel. And would you believe it – I never heard another word from Stone? What do you make of that?'

'I make that Mr. Stone was very eager to get Mr. Mackenzie out of the way so that Mrs. Mackenzie could get out of the Wendham. I make also that Mrs. Mackenzie prompted Mr. Stone's entire correspondence. There is always an accommodating laundress to receive mail, or a farmer's wife who brings around fresh eggs. . . . The decision to take Mrs. Mackenzie to New York probably upset the original plan. If Mr. Mackenzie had gone alone, he would perhaps not have heard from

76

Mr. Stone at all. Nor found Mrs. Mackenzie back on the farm in Edmonton.'

Mackenzie looked stupefied, then furious. 'What a fool I've been! I'll put Schroeder on her track – no matter what it costs! Where is Schroeder? I want to see him!'

We offered to take him to Schroeder's hotel. On the way out we stopped for the mail. Mackenzie tore open a letter and read it, a puzzled frown between his brows.

'What do you make of this?' he demanded, holding it out to me.

' "Darling Philip –" ' it began.

I looked up. 'For Schmidt?'

He held out the envelope. It was addressed to *Philip Schmidt, Care William R. Mackenzie, Hotel Nacional,* and bore a Cuban stamp.

'Perhaps I shouldn't have opened it, but – you understand. Read it,' he urged.

When I sent that wire to the boat I really meant to patch things up with Emilio and never see you again. But last night he was drunk again – terribly – Oh my darling this time I mean it. I will go away with you – Come at once. I need you. Love – love – love –

It seemed plain enough then. Schmidt had wanted to get to Havana. In some way he got wind of Mrs. Mackenzie's flight and played on Mackenzie's credulity and distress to work the trip. On the boat he received a cable from his *Senora* calling the deal off. Curtain for Mr. Schmidt.

I was so pleased with my perspicuity that I blurted it out, not thinking of the effect on Mackenzie. I suppose subconsciously I felt I was doing him a good turn. I didn't realize that all along he had been buoyed up by the hope and excitement of the chase. With the prop removed he was in a bad way. No use now in seeing Schroeder. No use in anything.

He seemed on the point of collapse and I did what I could for him. It was pitiful the way he clung to us. By nightfall Gwynn had a headache, but I went in and played cards with him. And the next morning, as the headache persisted, we started off without her for Morro Castle. He looked wretched and there was a feverish light in his eyes. As I look back now I can understand it. His manner became more and more curious. He carried a Panama hat; but although the sun was doing its tropical best, he refused to put it on. And under his arm he clutched a package as though it contained rubies. I remember, before we left, Gwynn moved the package and he jumped and took it away from her and held it on his lap until I was ready to go.

Clarence Cobb had sent us a Captain of the Militia to act as guide. As he walked around the outside of the fortress, Mackenzie kept asking about sharks. The Captain told us stories. Vivid stories. They seemed to have a horrible effect on Mackenzie, who kept peering into the water and insisting he saw sharks. I couldn't get him away from those rocks. And he asked me whether I thought there had been sharks when Schmidt went overboard. I assured him there were none.

'I hate to think – maybe there were sharks –' He shut his eyes and swayed. I begged him to put on his hat. I thought the sun was affecting him. But he continued to spot sharks and mumble about Schmidt – once excusing him: 'I can understand him. Why go on living without the one thing you want most?' and the next time cursing him: 'I had no reason for loving the – but if I had thought that there were sharks –'

The sentence stuck in my mind until I realised it was because of the tense. If he didn't know until yesterday. . . .

The Captain was telling us about the dungeons where tradition has embroidered fantastic tales of cruelty to prisoners.

79

Mackenzie shuddered and swayed again.

'Look here,' I said, 'if you'd rather not go in . . .?'

'Why shouldn't I?' He bridled. 'Why shouldn't I look at dungeons?' I wanted to get away. An idea had occurred to me. Since Mackenzie had opened Schmidt's letter, perhaps he had also opened that wire on the boat and read it. . . . Fury at Schmidt would supply a motive. . . . I wanted to talk it over with Gwynn.

There is nothing in those dungeons except what imagination paints into them. But we had no sooner stepped inside than Mackenzie had to go out again. We waited for him to return and then went in search of him. Back on the rocks where we had watched for sharks I saw something. I picked it up. It was a wallet monogrammed *W.R.M.* It had not fallen there. It had been wedged between the rocks – conspicuously – where searchers would not fail to find it.

I looked down at the graying water. A Panama hat floated on a wave. Was it imagination or did I see a dark fin cutting the surface of the water? . . . Suddenly the hat disappeared. I became violently ill.

The papers gave the story a great play. Suicide of Wealthy Canadian in Waters off Morro

Castle. . . . Eyewitness Sees Sharks Attack Hat. . . . Wm. R. Mackenzie, despondent over the loss of his wife, ended his life etc. . . . etc. . . . And they gave plenty of space to the wallet, which contained travelers' checks and a farewell note addressed to Mrs. Mackenzie.

'So I guess Mrs. Keats had the right hunch,' said Schroeder, 'and Mackenzie did finish Schmidt before he went up to the bar.'

'Quite a while before,' said Gwynn, and outlined what she thought had taken place. 'I figure he got him out on deck and possibly hit him over the head while he was leaning over the rail. The steward said the man was lying with his head on his arms and looked ghastly. Our boy friend may only have pretended to get an answer about the doctor. Maybe there was no answer. Watching his chance, he dropped him overboard. Then he went into the stateroom and fixed up Schmidt's suitcase – messed up the bed – rang for the steward and met him in the companionway to register that Schmidt was asleep. Then he went to the bar and began that wild orgy of treating, during which he proceeded to get so sick that he wouldn't have to go back into that cabin, or have anything to do with discovering Schmidt's absence. Or answer too many questions. And I daresay, when I dropped in, he was a little sorry he had been so friendly the night before.'

'Poor guy,' said I. 'Out of a boatload of people, he just had to pick on *you*. Author of Perfect Crime Makes One Fatal Error.'

'Author of *this* perfect crime made several. And something tells me it will eventually make good telling.'

'Eventually! Why not now?'

'I should say not! Think of my sense of drama. By the way, Mr. Schroeder, did you ever find out his wife's name?'

'Temple Mackenzie.'

'Temple –' said Gwynn musingly.

'Why?'

'It might be a good thing to remember.'

Back in New York, we received a phone call from Erik Schroeder. He was working on a big case and wanted Gwynn's hunch on it – the well-known woman's angle. At his apartment the talk naturally drifted to Mackenzie. Schroeder had followed up certain threads. 'You never can tell,' he jeered, 'I may want to write it up for the magazines.'

Gwynn laughed. 'Without a final chapter?'

'I think I have a tag –'

'Then you saw that bit in yesterday's paper?'

'What bit –?'

'From Hollywood?'

'What has Hollywood to do –'

'Pardon me, I spoke out of turn. What's your tag?'

'Well, far from being a rich man, the only estate Mackenzie left was his expectations from that patent which, unfortunately, isn't worth a damn. One of the G.E. men told me everything in it is covered by better patents of their own. You questioned his being a rich man. In fact, you called all the turns. Having read some of your fiction detectives, I should say Lady Novelist takes Great Detective for a ride all along the line – and that makes our last chapter.'

'Next to the last,' corrected Gwynn. 'You haven't by any chance seen "Wild Eagle" at the Paramount this week?'

'Don't change the subject,' said I. 'Stick to the Mackenzie tale.'

'That's it.'

'The picture you saw this afternoon? Don't be so damn' cryptic.'

'Can't a girl have her simple pleasures? Knowing we were going to see Mr. Schroeder I couldn't resist a sort of coup. My dramatic instinct, you know. I'll sit through the picture again for the pleasure of watching your faces. And then I'll tell you *my* final chapter.'

For two reels nothing happened. And then

Schroeder straightened up in his seat and I exclaimed aloud. . . . There on the screen in riding breeches was Wm. R. Mackenzie!

'The son-of-a-gun!' said Schroeder, when we were back in his apartment. 'I'll bet you got a shock when he walked on this afternoon.'

'Not exactly. I went there expressly to see him. But maybe I'd better go back and "tell all"?' inquired my wife brightly.

'Maybe you'd better,' replied her husband grimly.

'Remember the night you went to Philadelphia, Colin?' I did, of course. 'Well, it's a good thing you didn't call me because I wasn't home. I was out all night.'

I refrained from comment.

'I was at the Wendham. Took a room on the same floor on which the Mackenzies had stayed and got clubby with Helen, the chambermaid. She remembered Mrs. Mackenzie – a tall, pretty blonde It seems she had got clubby with Helen, too, and complained about Mackenzie . . . he had plenty of money but was terribly tight . . . kept her cooped up on a farm like a prisoner. "Of course," said Helen, "if she left him she wouldn't get a cent and he left her everything in his will. He made it before they were married. But she said to me, she said, 'What the hell! Money isn't everything.' "

'I'd been wondering how Temple managed to communicate with her lover.'

'How did you know she had a lover?' demanded Schroeder. 'Schmidt may have made up that whole business.'

'Oh, she had to have a lover, for my hunch. Anyway, the bathroom of the Mackenzie suite has a door into the next suite. Temple goes in, turns on a tub, and has ready communion with the gentleman in the next suite, whom, by the way, you saw tonight – the tall, curly-headed young man in breeches.'

'Hold everything! That one was Mackenzie –'

'The billing says Pat Salisbury,' Gwynn pointed out.

'Yes, but I thought Mackenzie had taken the name of Salisbury –'

'No – the other way round. Salisbury took the name of Mackenzie. After he murdered him and dropped him overboard.'

'By God!' Schroeder brought his fist down.

'Wait a minute!' I cried. 'I don't get you –'

'Take your time,' replied Gwynn. 'Or – I'll tell it to you by easy stages. I'd better begin three years ago – in Hollywood with a couple of young people named Temple Drury and Pat Salisbury – both working in pictures –

and the going pretty rough for the girl. Along comes Mackenzie – poses as a millionaire – even making out a will leaving her his fortune. Poor man thought he would have one, some day! She marries him and he takes her to Canada and keeps her cooped up while he monkeys with his invention. Having had a taste of starvation, maybe for a while she is grateful for the security of a roof and three squares. But eventually she gets restless and manages to communicate with the old boy-friend, Salisbury.

At last she decides to run away. But Mackenzie watches her like a hawk. So Salisbury, in New York on a little spree, writes the husband exactly the kind of letter that would interest him, signing it Paul Stone, and lures him to New York. But something about Temple's manner at the last minute worries Mackenzie and he decides to take her with him.

'Salisbury, who has been staying at the Wendham, and only picking up mail addressed to "Stone" at the Alamac, gets him a suite next to his. Temple and he perfect their plans through the bathroom door and he phones Mackenzie, as Paul Stone, of course, and sends him on a wild-goose chase up to the Alamac.

'He puts Temple in another hotel and,

knocking later at Mackenzie's door, introduces himself as Philip Schmidt, a detective. And he gets expense money from Mackenzie, which he turned over to Temple. . . . I trust.'

'Maybe his first idea was only to get a few thousand dollars from Mackenzie – string him along – and blow. But Mackenzie wasn't easy to pluck. And it probably seemed a pity that he and Temple should be broke – when that will left her all that money? If only Mackenzie were out of the way. . . .

'Salisbury worked out a pretty neat scheme. On a boat nobody knows who anybody is for the first day. The steward only knows that the two gentlemen in 361 are Mr. Mackenzie and Mr. Schmidt. And if one jumped overboard and the other claimed that Schmidt was missing – who would think it was Mackenzie who was gone? Whereas, if a wealthy man were to disappear under mysterious circumstances, investigation might involve his secretary. And certainly the wife would be questioned and her connection with Mr. Salisbury uncovered. But when Schmidt was missing even Mr. Schroeder asked: What motive would a man have for murdering his secretary?'

'Probably the ipecac which made the young man too sick for questioning also made Mackenzie too sick for talking. As soon as the boat starts, Salisbury-Stone-Schmidt puts Mackenzie to bed and does all the talking for the team – making out the poor man is a Scientist, so even the doctor won't be brought in.

'Then while the steward is freshening up the room, Salisbury gets the real Mackenzie on deck and finishes him. And from then on he has a fourth identity. He is now known as Wm. R. Mackenzie. And nobody questions that identity. Still, everything doesn't go as smoothly as Mr. Salisbury-Mackenzie would have liked. There is a snoopy detective on board and a very snoopy woman. They keep wanting a reason for Schmidt's suicide. So the young man supplies a reason – in a letter from a non-existent lady in Havana – without any address.

'When he went out to post that letter, by the way, was the only time he left the Nacional. You see, he didn't have any money. Unfortunately, all the real Mackenzie's money was in travelers' checks which he couldn't cash!

'Of course that letter from 'C' also provided a motive for a fit of despondency in which he could make it seem that Mackenzie had killed himself. Because for Temple to inherit Mackenzie's money, Mackenzie had to be legally dead. So Mackenzie apparently jumps into shark-infested waters – after a fine piece of acting by Mr. Salisbury-Mackenzie. Which suicide, incidentally, took care of the bill at the Nacional. On the waves floats the Panama hat which he never could wear because it was too small! On the rocks lie the travelers' checks, which will revert to Temple and be of *some* use – and a note to remove any possible doubt of his suicide.

'But there doesn't seem to have been any doubt. Only the package worried me. What could there have been in a package that a man would want to have with him when he set out to kill himself – with a suicide note all typed in his pocket? ... And what had become of it? Had he taken it with him?

'You know how those flashes come to you. Of course he had taken it with him ... out of the fortress ... a coat and a cap! Suppose Colin and the Captain had asked the guard – which they didn't, once they saw the note – about a blond hatless man in a Palm beach suit? Would they have connected him with a young man in, say, a blue serge coat, a cap pulled down over his hair, and perhaps dark glasses?'

Schroeder smoked in thoughtful silence. But I insisted on knowing, step by step, how she had hit on it.

'Oh, darling, you *are* such a perfect straight man! Sometimes you just smell a phony and begin to reason from the smell.'

'Or maybe you note little things,' smiled Schroeder, 'and then begin to sniff.'

'Maybe. . . . I knew I wouldn't get anything out of a Schroeder by asking, so I brought the talk around to it at Cobb's, and then we began to make a little headway. But a couple of times Salisbury threw me off – like when he told that long circumstantial story of Mrs. Mackenzie's elopement which Mr. Schroeder could check . . . and did.'

'Why do you suppose he told all that?' I demanded foggily.

'I think he was secretly proud of his scenario and was having fun with Schroeder and me. And I'm sure he was vain of his acting.'

'Not bad acting,' admitted Schroeder grudgingly. He smiled again, however.

'Excellent . . . only somebody else should have written his lines and left out the American slang. That was the first whiff I got . . . pure American idiom from a man who had only been in the States twice – on short visits!

'Anybody could have found out what I did at the Wendham . . . that Mackenzie was a middle-aged, darkish man . . . that

90

when the Mackenzies had Suite 805, 806 was occupied by a Pat Salisbury, registered from Hollywood . . . and anybody would have been impressed by the similarity of the initials . . . Pat Salisbury – Paul Stone – Philip Schmidt.

'And anybody would have written to Hollywood and found out that Wm. R. Mackenzie had married Temple Drury in June 1930 . . . that Temple Drury was listed at Central Casting among the extras . . . that she had one bit in a Fox picture and that Pat Salisbury had a part in the same opus . . . that his last rôle was a small one in "Wild Eagle," after which he left for New York. It was all there to put together – except where he got the money to get out of Havana and back to Temple.'

'A man as resourceful as Mr. Salisbury probably found a way,' suggested Schroeder.

'Not probably – actually. They even got out to Hollywood – although it must have been a blow to find that Mackenzie hadn't left any fortune.'

'How do you know he got to Hollywood?' asked Schroeder. 'That picture was made before he left for New York.'

'That,' said Gwynn, 'is the pay-off. I asked you whether you'd seen an item in the papers. I brought the clipping with me.'

91

ACTOR AND WIFE KILLED

Mr. and Mrs. Pat Salisbury were instantly killed when their car crashed through a railing on a sharp turn of Topanga Pass. The car had been rented by the young couple for the day. Pat Salisbury was last seen in 'Wild Eagle' – a Paramount Picture. Mrs. Salisbury was formerly Temple Drury. The couple had not found work since their recent return to Hollywood. Police are investigating the theory of a suicide pact.

MIGNON EBERHART

Susan Dare in
Easter Devil

Susan Dare sipped her coffee and quietly contemplated devils. Outside, rain beat down upon cold, dark streets, and inside the drawn curtains of Susan's small library it was warm, with a fire cheerful in the grate, and the dog lazy upon the rug, and cigarettes and an old book beside the deepest armchair. An armchair which Susan just then decorated, for she had dressed for her dinner *à seul* in soft trailing crimson. Too bad, thought Susan regretfully, that her best moments were so often wasted; a seductive crimson gown, and no one to see it. She smashed her cigarette sadly and returned to her book.

Devils and devil-possessed souls! Of course there were no such things, but it was curious how real the old writers made both.

Then the doorbell rang. The dog barked and scrambled to his feet and bounced into the hall, and Susan followed.

Two men, beaten and wet with rain, were

93

waiting, and one of them was Jim Byrne, with a package under his arm.

'Company?' asked Jim tersely looking at the dress.

'No. I was alone –'

'You remember Lieutenant Mohrn?'

Of course she did! It was her volunteer work with him on a recent Chicago crime that had led the police force to regard her as a valuable consultant.

'How do you do?' said Lieutenant Mohrn. 'I hope you don't mind our coming. You see, there's something –'

'Something queer,' said Jim. 'In point of fact, it's –'

'Murder,' said Lieutenant Mohrn.

'Oh,' said Susan. Her own small warm house – and these two men with sober faces looking at her. She smoothed back her hair. 'Oh,' she said again.

Jim pushed the package toward her.

'I got size thirty-six,' he said. 'Is that right? – I mean, that's what we want you to wear.'

That was actually Susan's introduction to the case of the Easter Devil. Fifteen minutes later she was getting out of the glamorous crimson gown and into a brown tweed suit with a warm topcoat, and tossing a few things into a bag – the few things included the contents of the package, which proved to be several nurses' uniforms, complete with caps, and a small set of instruments which were new and shiny.

'Do you know anything about nursing?' Jim Byrne had asked.

'Nothing,' said Susan. 'But I've had appendicitis.'

'Oh,' said Jim relieved. 'Then you can – oh, take a pulse, make a show of nursing. She's not sick, you know. If she were, we could not do this.'

'I can shake a thermometer without dropping it,' said Susan. 'If the doctor will help –'

'Oh, he'll help all right,' said Lieutenant Mohrn somewhat grimly. 'We have his consent and approval.'

She pulled a small brown hat over her hair and then remembered to change gold slippers to brown oxfords.

In the hall Jim was waiting.

'Mohrn had to go,' he said. 'I'll take you out. Glenn Ash is about an hour's run from town.'

'All right,' said Susan. She scribbled a note to Huldah and spoke soberly to the dog, who liked to have things explained to him.

'I'm going to a house in Glenn Ash,' she said gravely. 'Be a good dog. And don't chase the neighbour's cat.'

He pushed a cold nose against her hand. He didn't want her to go, and he thought the matter of Petruchkin the cat might better have been ignored. Then the front door closed and he heard presently two doors bang and a car drive away. He returned to the library. But he was gradually aware that the peace and snugness were gone. He felt gloomily that it would have been very much better if the woman had stayed at home.

And the woman, riding along a rainswept road, rather agreed with him. She peered through the rain-shot light lanes ahead and reviewed in her mind the few facts she knew. And they were brief enough.

At the home of one Gladstone Denisty in Glenn Ash a servant had been murdered. Had been shot in the back and found (where he'd fallen) in a ravine near the house. There was no weapon found, and anyway he couldn't have shot himself. There were no signs of attempted burglary. There were, indeed, no clues. He was a quiet, well-behaved man and an efficient servant and had been with the Denisty family for some time; so far as could be discovered, his life held no secrets.

Yet that morning he had been found in the ravine, murdered.

The household consisted of Gladstone Denisty and his wife; his mother and brother, and two remaining servants.

'It's Mrs. Gladstone Denisty – her first name is Felicia – whom we want you to nurse,' Lieutenant Mohrn had said. 'There's more to the thing than meets the eye. You see, the only lead we have leads to the Denisty home; this man was killed by a bullet of the same calibre as that of a revolver which is known to have been in the Denisty house – property of nobody in particular – and which has disappeared within the last week. But that's all we know. And we thought if we could get you inside the house – just to watch things, you know. There's no possible danger to you.'

'There's always danger,' said Jim brusquely, 'where there's murder.'

'If Miss Dare thinks there's danger, she's to leave,' said Lieutenant Mohrn wearily. 'All I want her to do is get a – line on things.'

And Jim, somehow grudgingly, had said nothing; still said nothing.

It was a long ride to Glenn Ash, and that night a difficult one, owing to the rain and wind. But they did finally turn off the winding side road into a drive and stop.

Susan could barely see the great dark bulk of the house looming above with only a light or two showing.

Then Jim's hand was guiding her up some brick steps and across a wide veranda. He put his mouth to her ear: 'If anything happens that you don't like, leave. At once.' And Susan whispered, 'I will,' and Jim was gone, and the wide door was opening, and a very pretty maid was taking her bag and leading her swiftly upstairs. The household had retired, said the maid, and Mrs. Denisty would see her in the morning.

'You mean Mrs. Gladstone Denisty?' asked Susan.

'Oh, no, ma'am. *Mrs. Denisty,*' said the maid. 'Is there anything –? Thank you. Good night, ma'am.'

Susan, after a thoughtful moment, locked her door and presently went to bed and listened to the rain against the windowpanes and wished she could sleep. However, she must have fallen asleep, for she woke up suddenly and in fright. It had stopped raining. And somewhere there had been a sound.

There had been a sound, but it was no more. She only knew that it had waked her and that she was ridiculously terrified. And then all at once her heart stopped its absurd pounding and was perfectly still. For something – out there in the long and empty hall – had brushed against her bedroom door!

She couldn't, either then or later, have

persuaded herself to go to that door and open it and look into the hall. And anyway, as the moments dragged on, she was convinced that whoever or whatever had brushed against her door was gone. But she sat, huddled under blankets, stonily wide awake until slow grey dawn began to crawl into the room. Then she fell again into sleep, only to be wakened this time by the maid, carrying a breakfast tray and looking what she thought of trained nurses who slept late. Mrs. Denisty, she informed Susan, wished to see her.

Not, thought Susan, getting into the unaccustomed uniform, an auspicious beginning. And she was shocked to discover that she looked incredibly young and more than a little flip in the crisply tailored white dress and white cap. She took her horn-rimmed spectacles, which improved things very little, and her thermometer, and went downstairs, endeavouring to look stern enough to offset the unfortunate effect of the cap.

But on the wide landing of the stairs she realized that the thick, white-haired woman in the hall below was interested only in the tongue-lashing she was giving two maids. They were careless, they were lying, they had broken it – all of it. She looked up just then and saw Susan and became at once bland.

'Good morning, Miss Dare,' she said. 'Will you come down? She dismissed the servants and met Susan at the foot of the stairs. 'We'll go into this drawing-room,' she said. She wore a creamy white wool dress with blue beads and a blue handkerchief and did not ask Susan to sit down.

'The household is a little upset just now,' she said. 'There was an unfortunate occurrence here, night before last. Yes – unfortunate. And then yesterday or last night the maid or cook or somebody managed to break some Venetian glass – quite a lot of it – that my daughter-in-law was much attached to. Neither of them will admit it. However, about my daughter-in-law, Mrs. Gladstone Denisty, whom you are here to care for: I only wished to tell you, Miss Dare, that her nerves are bad, and the main thing, I believe, is merely to humour her. And if there is anything you wish to know, or if any – problem – arises, come to me. Do you understand?'

Susan wondered what was wrong with the room and said she understood.

'Very well,' said Mrs. Denisty, rising. 'That is all.'

But that was not all. For there was a whirlwind of steps, and a voice sobbing broken phrases swept through the door, and a woman ran into the room clutching in both hands something bright and crimson. A queer little chill that she could never account for crept over Susan as she realized that the woman clutched, actually, broken pieces of glass.

'Did you see, Mother Denisty?' sobbed the woman. 'It's all over the floor. How much more – how much more –'

'Felicia!' cried Mrs. Denisty sternly. 'Hush – yes, I know. It was an accident.'

'An accident! But you know – you know –'

'The nurse is here – Miss Dare.'

The young woman whirled. she was – or had been – of extraordinary beauty. Slender and tall, with fine, fair hair and great, brilliant grey eyes. But the eyes were hollow and the lids swollen and pink, and her mouth pale and uncertain.

'But I don't need a nurse.'

'Just for a few days,' said Mrs. Denisty firmly. 'The doctor advised it.'

The great grey eyes met Susan's fixedly – too fixedly, indeed, for the look was actually an unwavering stare. Was there something, then, beyond Susan – near Susan – that she did not wish to see?

'*Oh,*' said Felicia Denisty with a thin sharp gasp and looked at her hand, and Susan ran forward. On the slender white hand was a brighter, thicker crimson than the Venetian

101

glass which was just then and quite slowly relinquished.

'You've cut your hand,' said Susan inadequately. Felicia had turned to the older woman, who was unmoved.

'See,' she said, extending her bleeding hand. 'Just to be in the room with it –'

Mrs. Denisty moved forward then.

'Will you go upstairs with Mrs. Gladstone, Miss Dare,' she said firmly, 'and dress her hand.'

Upstairs Susan blessed a brief course of Red Cross lectures which during school days she had loathed, and made a fairly workmanlike job of bandaging the wound.

But it was not so easy to spend the long hours of the slow grey day with Felicia Denisty, for she had fallen into a brooding silence, sat and stared either at her bandaged hand or out of the window upon a dreary balcony, and said practically nothing.

The afternoon passed much as the morning, except that with the approach of dusk the wind rose a bit and rattled shutters, and Felicia grew restless and turned on every available light in her room.

'Dinner,' she said to Susan, 'is at seven-thirty.' She looked fully at Susan, as if for the first time. 'You've been inside all day, Miss

Dare. I didn't think – would you like to take a walk before dinner?'

Susan said she would, and hoped she wasn't too eager.

But at the end of half an hour's walk through rapidly increasing grey dusk, she was still no wiser than she had been, except that she had a clearer notion of the general plan of the house – built like a wide-flung T with tall white pillars running up to the second-story roof of the wide double porch, which extended across the front of the house – and of the grounds.

On two sides of the house was a placid brown lawn, stretching downward to roadway and to rolling meadows. But on the south lay the ravine, an abrupt irregular gash, masked now and made mysterious by dripping shrubbery. Beyond it appeared the roof of a house, and at the deepest point of the ravine it was crossed by a small wooden bridge which lost itself in the trees at the farther end. It must lead, thought Susan, to the house, but she did not explore it, although she looked at the spot where (as revealed by a discreet inquiry of the pretty housemaid) the butler had been murdered.

It was perhaps ten feet from the entrance to the small wooden bridge and just behind a large clump of sumach. It was not in view from the windows of the Denisty house.

Susan, made oddly uneasy by the fog-enshrouded shadows of the trees, made her way back.

Once inside she turned at once to the drawing-room. It was dark, and she fumbled for the light and found it. The room was exactly as she remembered it from the morning; a large room of spaces and many windows and massive furniture. Not somehow a pleasant room. It was too still, perhaps, too chilly, too – she turned suddenly as if someone had spoken her name and saw the Easter image.

And she realized what was wrong with the room.

'It stood there beside the fireplace – a black, narrow image of a man – a terribly emaciated man, with protruding ribs and a queer, painted face, roughly carved. It was perhaps two feet tall and there were white marks on it that looked like, but were not, chalk. Its emaciation and its protruding ribs suggested that it was a remnant of that strangely vanished race from mysterious, sombre Easter Island. When you looked at it analytically, that was all there was to see.

But it was singularly difficult to look at it analytically. And that was because of the curiously repellent look in its face; the air of strange and secret sentience that somehow managed to surround the small figure. There was a hint of something decadent, something faintly macabre, something incredibly and hideously wise. It was intangible: it was not sensible. But, nevertheless, it was there.

Yet, Susan told herself sternly, the image itself was merely a piece of wood.

A carved piece of wood from Easter Island; a souvenir, probably, of a journey there. It had no connection with the murder of a butler, with the shattered fine fragments of Venetian glass.

Susan turned suddenly and left the drawing-room. But when in the hall the door behind her opened, Susan all but screamed before she saw the man who had entered. He flung off hat and coat and reached for a stack of letters on the hall table and then finally looked up at her and said: 'Oh, hullo. You must be the nurse. Miss –'

'Dare,' said Susan. He was thick, white-haired, brusque, with a blunt nose and bright, hard blue eyes. He wasn't over forty-five, and he must be a Denisty.

'Dare,' he said. 'Nice name. Well, take care of my wife.' His blue eyes shot a quick glance up the stairway, and he bent and kissed at Susan; turned, humming, toward the library, and vanished.

Kissed at her; for what she felt would have been a rather expert kiss had been pretty well deflected by some quick action on her part.

Well, that was Gladstone.

And Marlowe Denisty, the brother, who turned up at dinner, was a handsome Byronic-looking youth who talked enthusiastically of practically everything.

It was Marlowe who later, in the drawing-room, spoke of the Easter image.

He had brought it, he told Susan expansively, from Easter Island himself. It was a present to Gladstone.

'An akuaku,' said Susan absently.

'A *what?*' said Gladstone, turning sharply to look at her.

Susan wished she had not spoken, and Marlowe flashed her a glance of bright approval.

'An akuaku,' he said. 'An evil god. You remember, Glad, I told you all about it when I brought the thing home. These wooden figures, or moai miro, were made first, so far as can be discovered, by Tuukoihu, who ruled the island following Hotu Matua. These small figures with protruding ribs were thought to be reminders of the imminence of death, threats of –'

'Thank you, I can read the encyclopaedia

myself,' said Gladstone Denisty sharply. 'And anyway, it's all nonsense. A piece of carved wood with white painting on it can't possibly have any sort of significance.'

'It *can* have,' cried Felicia with sudden unexpected violence. 'It *does* have!'

Mrs. Denisty, with a glance at Gladstone, interrupted. 'Felicia, dear child,' she cried in a deprecating way. 'How can you be so absurd!'

'Hush!' Felicia's voice was all at once taut; her eyes were wide and dark, and she flung out her hand toward the image. 'Don't you realize that it hears you? Don't you realize what it has brought into this house? Misfortune – suffering – murder –'

'Felicia!' The interruption was loud and covered anything Felicia might have continued to say, and Mrs. Denisty went on swiftly: 'You are hysterical, my dear, and not quite yourself. As to misfortune, we have lost no more than other people and are still very comfortable. And your illness couldn't possibly have been induced by a wooden image –'

'An evil god – an evil influence,' muttered Felicia staring at the image.

Mrs. Denisty swept on, though her mouth was tight.

'And William's death, which I suppose

you are referring to, was the result of his discovering an attempt to burgle the house. It is dreadful of course. But it had no possible connection with this – this piece of wood.'

Felicia was trembling. Susan put a hand upon her arm but could not stay the uneven torrent of words.

'What of the things that have happened to me? – Why, even my kitten died. Flowers die if I touch them. Something happens to everything that is mine. Why – just last night – the glass –' She was sobbing. 'William – he was kind to me – he –'

Gladstone intervened.

'Take her upstairs, Miss Dare,' he said quietly. 'See if you can quiet her. She has some capsules the doctor gave her – try to calm yourself, Felicia.'

'Oh, I'll go. I'll go.'

She sobbed weakly. But she said no more, and once in her room upstairs took the sedative and afterwards lay quiet, staring at the ceiling with great tragic eyes.

'Your illness,' said Susan gently. 'The doctor didn't tell me –'

Felicia did not look at her.

'Nerves, he says. That's all any of them say. But I as all right until he brought the image home. About a year ago.' The sedative was beginning to take effect, and she spoke calmly. 'It is the image, you see, Miss Dare. It hates me. I feel it. I know it. And – I heard the story – of a woman in Tahiti, an Englishwoman, who had one, and it hated her, and it brought evil and suffering and misfortune, and finally – death.'

She spoke the last word in a whisper.

Did Marlowe tell you of it?'

'Yes. He told us. We thought nothing of it – then. Mother Denisty says it is wrong of me to fear it. She's religious, you know.'

'She holds very firmly to the church?'

'Oh, yes. Except in the modern trend. That is – divorce, you know. She is very much against divorce.' Owing perhaps to the capsule, Felicia was beginning to talk in a rambling way. 'She says my feeling about the image is superstition.'

'How was William kind to you?' asked Susan.

'Oh, in so many little ways. I think he liked me. It was he who told me about the flowers. Of course, I didn't believe him. I know why they died. But he told me that, so I would feel better.' She was becoming drowsy, and her words were soft and slow.

Susan felt and stifled with rather shocking ease a scruple against further questions and said: 'What did he tell you?'

'Oh – something about acid in the water.

I don't know – it couldn't have been true. Flowers died because they were mine. And I don't want to study French any more.'

'*French,*' said Susan. '*French!*'

Felicia's drooping eyelids flared open. She stared hazily but intently at Susan and suddenly lifted herself on one elbow and leaned toward her and whispered hoarsely: 'It's Dorothy. She knows about the image. I can see it in her eyes. In her eyes.' She dropped back upon the pillow, repeated: 'In her eyes – in her eyes,' and then quite suddenly was heavily asleep.

After a long time Susan tiptoed away.

But at midnight she was still broadly awake, strongly aware, as one is at night, of the house about her and all that it held – including the thing that brooded over a downstairs room.

Only a piece of wood.

And what possible connection was there between a piece of wood, some shattered fine glass, and a murdered butler? French lessons and dead flowers and an acid? A kitten – dead also. An image that represented the imminence of death. A hysterical woman – talking of death.

That night, if anyone brushed against her door, Susan did not know it, for she fell at length into an uneasy sleep.

Her second day in the Denisty household

was in many ways a replica of the first, except that nothing at all happened.

Once during the morning she heard Mrs Denisty telephoning to someone she called Dorothy and saying that Felicia would not be able to do French that morning, which left Susan little wiser than she had been. And once she herself was called to the telephone for what proved to be an extremely guarded conversation with Jim Byrne. She succeeded only in reassuring him as to her own personal safety, told him carefully that she did not know how long the 'case' would last, and hung up.

That night, too, was quiet. But the next day things happened.

In the first place, 'Dorothy' came to call. Susan, just entering Felicia's room with the morning paper, heard her voice on the stairs.

'Is Mrs Gladstone in her room?'

'Yes, Mrs. Laasch,' replied the housemaid's voice.

'So I thought. No, no – I know the way. Mrs Gladstone won't mind.'

Susan waited. In another moment the owner of the voice came along the hall, glanced at Susan, and preceded her into Felicia's room with the ease of very old and intimate acquaintance.

'Oh, good morning, Dorothy,' said Felicia.

111

So this was Dorothy. Dorothy Laasch. Susan gave Felicia the paper and at Felicia's gesture sat down near her.

'Mother Denisty tells me there'll be no more French until you are feeling better,' Dorothy was saying. She was a handsome woman in perhaps her middle thirties; a blonde with short hair, vivacious if rather large features, and light, swift eyes. She wore a green wool suit, no hat, and suede pumps. Felicia murmured something and Dorothy went on:

'Since Mother Denisty says so, I suppose that settles it. You ought to rouse yourself, Felicia. You let that woman rule you. Just because she controls the purse strings –'

'Dorothy,' said Felicia in a remonstrating way.

Dorothy shot a quick glance toward the door into the hall.

'She's outdoors. I met her down by the bridge.'

'But –' said Felicia.

'Oh, you mean the nurse.' Dorothy looked at Susan and laughed. 'Nurses neither hear nor care, do they, Miss –'

'Dare,' said Felicia. She turned briefly to Susan. 'This is Mrs. Laasch. I thought you'd met. Let's put off the French lessons for a couple of weeks, Dorothy.'

'Nonsense,' said Dorothy vigorously. 'You'll be all right in a day or two. How's Mother Denisty taking this business of William's death?'

'I – don't know,' faltered Felicia.

'No, I don't suppose you do know,' said Dorothy with something like exasperation. 'Really, Felicia, you can't see anything. Have the police done anything?'

'About William, you mean? Nothing more. At least, nothing that I know of.'

Dorothy patted Felicia's hand briskly.

'Then why do you worry? Mother Denisty can't live for ever. And think of the insurance she –'

'Mother Denisty is very kind to me,' said Felicia. Her hands were trembling.

'Kind,' said Dorothy. She laughed abruptly. 'You are all afraid of her. Every one of –'

'Ah, there you are, Dorothy,' said Mrs. Denisty's bland voice from the doorway. Dorothy turned quickly, Felicia bent closer over her knitting, and Susan felt quite suddenly as if something had shifted and moved under her feet. Like quicksand, she thought, only it was nothing so perceptible.

'I hope you've cheered up Felicia,' said Mrs. Denisty. Her eyes were as blank and cold as two blue beads, but her voice was pleasant. If she had heard Dorothy's words, she gave no indication of it.

'I've tried to,' said Dorothy. She rose. 'I must run now. Good-bye, Felicia. Good-bye, Miss Dare. Good-bye, Mother Denisty.'

She kissed Felicia's white face; she kissed Mrs. Denisty. But Susan rose and walked downstairs and out by the wide front door with Dorothy, who accepted her company with the breezy manner that seemed characteristic of her.

'Poor Felicia,' said Dorothy. 'Do walk along to the bridge with me, Miss Dare. The path goes this way. I live just across the ravine, you know. I should be so alone but for Felicia. I'm a widow, you know. Tell me, just how *is* Felicia?'

'She seems not much changed,' said Susan.

'That's what I feared. It seems so queer and useless for her to brood over William. I can't imagine –' She checked herself abruptly and then continued in the same rapid way: 'I don't believe any of them realize the state Felicia is in. And Miss Dare – I am afraid for her.'

'Afraid? Of whom?'

Dorothy paused before she said, very slowly: 'I'm afraid Felicia has Felicia to fear more than anyone else.'

Suicide! Brooding over William. Was that what Dorothy meant? At their right was the patch of brown, dripping sumach. Susan said: 'That's where the man was murdered, isn't it?'

'About there, I believe,' said Dorothy. She met Susan's eyes for a long moment. 'Take care of Felicia – watch her, Miss Dare. Good-bye.'

Her heels tapped the wooden floor of the bridge. Susan watched, thinking of her last words, until Dorothy's blonde head vanished round the curve in the path beyond the bridge. Then Susan turned. As she did so something about the floor of the bridge caught her eye, and she bent to look.

Presently she rose and very thoughtfully went back to the house. But it was exactly then that terror clutched at Susan and would not be shaken off.

Yet, at the moment, there was nothing at all that she could do. Nothing but wait and listen and look.

It made it no easier when, that dreary afternoon, Felicia talked of death. Talked absently, queerly knitting a yellow afghan. What did Susan think it would be – did she think it would be difficult – would one regret at the last – when it was too late – would one –

'Has anyone talked to you – of death?' asked Susan sharply.

'N-no,' said Felicia. 'That is, Dorothy and I have talked of it. Some. And Marlowe always likes to discuss such things.'

'But that is wrong,' said Susan abruptly. 'You are sad and depressed.'

'Perhaps,' said Felicia agreeably. She knitted a long row before she said:

'Dear Glad – he is so good to me. He would, really, give me anything I want. Why, he would even give me a divorce if I asked for it: he has often said so. Not that I want a divorce. It only shows that he would put my wishes, even about that, ahead of Mother Denisty's.'

'Then why,' said Susan very gently, 'does he keep the – Easter image?'

Felicia flinched visibly, but replied:

'Why, you see, Miss Dare, he – he believes in its power. And he keeps it because he says it would be very weak to give in to his feeling about it.'

'But he talks as if –' began Susan irrepressibly and checked herself.

'Oh, yes,' said Felicia. 'But that's only because he doesn't like to admit it to other people.'

It was that night that the thing happened in the drawing-room. And that was the matter of the yellow afghan.

116

While they were at dinner, somehow, some time, under the very eyes of the Easter image, the knitting was unravelled.

They found it when they entered the chill and quiet drawing-room immediately after dinner. It lay in an untidy heap of crinkly yellow yarn, half on the chair where Felicia had left it, half on the floor.

Felicia saw it first and screamed.

And even Mother Denisty looked grey when she saw the heap of yarn. But she turned at once commandingly to Susan and told her to take Felicia upstairs.

Gladstone took Felicia's arm, and Susan followed, and somehow they got her out of the room. As they passed the still, black Easter image Felicia shuddered.

Upstairs, however, she managed to reply to Gladstone's inquiries.

Yes, she said, she had left the knitting there on the chair just before dinner.

'You are sure, Felicia?'

'Why, of course. I knew we would come into the drawing-room for coffee and I – I wanted to have my knitting there. It – keeps me from looking at the image –

'Nonsense, Felicia. The image won't hurt you.'

Felicia wrung her hands.

'Glad, don't keep up this pretence. You

117

know you are afraid of it, too. And Miss Dare knows –'

'Miss Dare –' He turned, his eyes blue and cold and exactly like his mother's, plunged into Susan's eyes and Felicia cried:

'So there's no need to pretend because she is here.'

'My wife,' said Gladstone to Susan, 'seems to be a bit hysterical –'

'Oh, no, no,' moaned Felicia. Don't you see? Listen to me, Glad.' She was leaning forward, two scarlet spots in her cheeks and her great eyes blazing. 'I left the knitting there in the chair. I was the last one in the dining-room – do you remember?'

'Y-yes,' said Gladstone unwillingly.

'No one left the table. No one was in the drawing-room. And when I returned, it was completely unravelled. Oh, it isn't the knitting that matters: I don't care about that. But it's the – the cruelty. The –' she paused searching for the word, wringing her hands again. Finally it came: 'The persecution,' said Felicia Denisty.

'Nonsense,' said Gladstone heavily. 'You are making too much of an absurdly trivial thing. Now, Felicia, do be sensible. Take one of your capsules and go to sleep. The image simply couldn't have pulled your knitting loose – if that's what you mean.'

'The image,' said Felicia slowly, 'couldn't have killed William, either. But William is dead.'

'Don't be morbid, Felicia,' said Gladstone. He paused with his hand on the door-knob. 'Miss Dare, will you help me a moment, please?'

It was, of course, an absurdly transparent excuse. Felicia said nothing and Susan followed Gladstone into the hall. He closed the door.

'Did my wife unravel the knitting herself, Miss Dare?' he said directly.

'I don't know.'

His hard blue eyes, so strangely like his mother's, were plumbing her own eyes, seeking for any thought that lay behind them.

'She seems to have been talking to you a great deal,' he said, slowly.

'No,' said Susan quietly, 'not a great deal.'

He waited for her to say more. But Susan waited, too.

'I hope,' he said at length, 'that you realize to what her talk is due.'

Susan smoothed back her hair.

'Yes,' she said truthfully. 'I believe I do.'

He stared at her again, then suddenly turned away.

'That's good,' he said. 'Good night, Miss Dare.'

He went down the stairs at once. In a moment, Susan heard the heavy outside door close. He had not, then, joined his mother and Marlowe, whose voices, steadily and blandly talking, were coming from the drawing-room. The room where the Easter image brooded and waited. She returned to Felicia.

'I took two capsules,' said Felicia wearily. 'You needn't stay, Miss Dare. I'll be asleep in no time.'

Two capsules. Susan resolved to talk to the doctor the next day, did what she could for Felicia, and left. This time she met Marlowe, his arms full of yellow wool.

'Oh, hello there, Miss Dare,' he said. 'I was just looking for you. What shall we do with this? Mother is frightfully upset about it. Glad is the apple of her eye, you know. It's never been exactly a happy marriage – you've probably guessed it. Poor mother. And now Felicia's got this queer notion about the Easter image.'

'How did she get the notion?' said Susan. 'I mean – has it been long?'

'M-m – a few months. Seems to have got worse since these unlucky things have been happening. Just accidents, of course. But it is a bit queer. Isn't it?'

'Very,' said Susan. 'Tell me, is she interested in the French lessons?'

120

'With Dorothy, you mean? Oh, I don't know. She goes regularly, nine o'clock every morning. Mother sees to that. But I don't know that she likes it much. Funny thing, psychology, isn't it? I suppose you see a lot of queer things in your profession, don't you?'

'Well,' said Susan guardedly, 'yes and no. Good night. Oh, I don't think it would be a good thing to give the yarn to her just now. Anyway, she's asleep.'

He turned toward the stairway, his arms still full of yellow yarn.

In her room, Susan locked the door as she had done carefully every night in the silent haunted house. Haunted by a wooden image.

And then, vehemently, she rejected the thought. It was no wooden image that menaced that house and those within it. It was something far stronger.

And yet she was shaken in spite of herself by the incident of the knitting. After all, *had* Felicia herself unravelled it? The family were all at the table and no one left it even momentarily. And the pretty housemaid who was, since William's death, acting as waitress, had been busily occupied and also, naturally, the cook.

But Susan was dealing only with intangibles. There was still no definite, material clue.

121

She turned, smoothed back her hair, and sat down at the writing desk. And set herself to reducing intangibles to tangibles.

It was after midnight when she leaned back and looked at what she had written.

A conclusion was there, of course, implicit in those facts. But she needed one link. And, even with that one link, she had no proof. Susan turned off the light and opened the window and stood there for a moment, looking out into the starless, quiet night.

Through the darkness and quiet a small dull sound came, beating with rhythmic little thuds upon her ears. And quite suddenly it was as if a small far-away tom-tom was beating out its dark and secret message.

Easter Island and a devil.

'This,' said Susan firmly to herself, 'is fantastic. The sound is made by footsteps on the wooden bridge.'

She listened, and faintly the footsteps came nearer. She could see nothing through the soft damp blackness. But suddenly, not far below her window, the footsteps ceased. Whoever was on the bridge then had now reached the path.

There was no way to know who had passed.

Yet quite suddenly Susan knew as surely as if she had seen.

And with the knowledge came the strangest

feeling of urgency. For she knew, with a blinding flash of light, what those footsteps on the bridge meant.

She snatched a dark silk dressing gown and flung it round her shoulders, unlocked her door and fled down the hall. She waited in the dusk above the stair railing, until the door below opened and she caught a glimpse of the person who entered. It was as she expected, and she turned and was at Felicia's door by the time the steps began to ascend the stairs.

If Felicia's door were locked! But it was not. She opened it and slipped inside and leaned against it, her heart pounding as if she'd been racing. Felicia was sleeping quietly and peacefully.

Now what to do? If there were only time – time to plan, time to make arrangements. But there was not.

And she had no proof.

And the feeling of urgency was stronger.

Felicia lay so sunk in sleep that only her heavy drugged breathing told Susan that she was alive.

At the bedside table was a telephone – a delicate gold and ivory thing – resting on a cradle.

Did she dare use it?

She must take the risk. She would need help.

She went to the telephone, lifted it, and called a number very softly into the ivory mouthpiece, and waited.

'Hello – hello –' It was Jim Byrne's voice and sounded sleepy and far away.

'Jim – Jim, this is Susan.'

'Susan – do you want me?'

'Yes.' Did she imagine it or did the floor creak very softly just below the door? If anyone were out there, if her voice, not Felicia's, were heard.

'Susan – what are you doing? *Susan* –'

Even at a distance the vibration from the telephone might be heard.

'Susan!' cried Jim and very softly Susan replaced the telephone on its cradle. Suddenly his voice was gone. And he was miles and miles away.

The floor under the door did not creak again. If she could only have told Jim what to do, what she was trying to do, where to wait until she signalled. Well, the thing now was to get Felicia out of danger.

She turned to the bed.

It was terrifically difficult to rouse Felicia. Susan was exhausted and trembling by the time she had managed to half carry and half push Felicia into the small dressing-room. A chaise-longue was there, and when Felicia's slack, inert figure collapsed upon it gracefully, she fell again into the horribly heavy slumber from which she had never fully aroused. And all the time there had been that dreadful necessity for haste.

Susan, panting from the sheer physical strain, very softly closed the door of the dressing-room.

Then, with the utmost caution, she turned the shade of the light so that it would not fall directly upon the door into the hall and yet so that anyone entering the room would be obliged to cross that narrow band of light.

Then, because she was shaking from cold and nerves and the strain of the past few moments, she took Felicia's place on the bed. And waited.

And in the waiting, as always happens, she became uncertain. All the other possibilities crowded into her mind. She was mistaken. There was no proof. This attempt to trap the murderer would fail. She was wrong in thinking that the attack would be made that night.

She knew that Jim Byrne, and probably Lieutenant Mohrn and a number of extremely active and husky policemen, were at that very moment speeding along the road to Glenn Ash.

The thought of it was inexpressibly comforting. But it was also fraught with dangerous possibilities. They might easily arrive too soon. They couldn't arrive too late, she thought, as, once she had proof, that was enough.

But there were so many ways the thing could go wrong, thought Susan rather desperately as the minutes ticked away on the little French clock on the mantle. And her own rapidly conceived plan was so weak, so full of loopholes, so dependent upon chance. Or was it?

After all, it had been intuitional, swift, certain. And intuition with her, Susan reminded herself firmly, was actually a matter of subconscious reasoning. And subconscious reasoning, she went on still firmly, was far better than conscious, rule-of-thumb reasoning. And anyway, the rule-of-thumb reasoning was clear too.

The attack upon Felicia must come. It had already been prepared and ready once, but then William, poor William, had come into it and interfered and had to be murdered.

She was in the deep shadow, there on Felicia's bed. But the door into the hall was in deep shadow, too. Would she hear it when it opened?

How long was it since she had telephoned

to Jim? Where was he now? What would he do when he arrived?

She became more and more convinced that the police would arrive too soon.

Yet, unless she was entirely mistaken, the attack must come soon. Although planned perhaps for months, that night it would be in one way an impulsive act.

She did not shift her eyes from the door. It was so quiet in the house – so terribly quiet and so cold. It was as if the Easter image downstairs had extended the realm of his possession. So cold –

It was then that Susan realized that the cold was coming from the window and that it was being opened, moving almost silently inward. Her eyes had jerked that way, and her heart gave a great leap of terror, but otherwise she had not moved.

She hadn't thought of the window.

A figure, black in the shadow, was moving with infinite stealth over the sill.

From the porch, of course, thought one part of Susan's mind. There are stairs somewhere; there must be. And then she realized coldly what a dangerous thing she had undertaken to do.

But it was done, and there she was in Felicia's place. And she must get one clear glimpse of that figure's face.

It was so dark in the shadows by the window. Susan realized that she must close her eyes and did so, feigning sleep and listening with taut nerves.

A rustle and a pause.

It was more than flesh and blood could bear. Surely that figure was far enough away from the window by this time so that it could not escape before Susan had a look at its face.

She moved, and there was still silence. She flung one arm outward lazily and sat up as if sleepily and opened her eyes.

'Is that you, Mrs. Denisty?' she asked drowsily.

And looked at the figure and directly into a revolver.

There was to be no pretence then. Susan's vague plan of talk, of excuses on both sides collapsed.

'If you shoot,' she said in a clear low voice that miraculously did not tremble, 'the whole house will be here before you can escape.'

'I know that.' The reply was equally low and clear. 'But you know too much, my dear.'

The last thing Susan remembered before that pandemonium of struggle began was the revolver being placed quite deliberately upon the green satin eiderdown. Then all knowledge was lost, and she was fighting – fighting for balance, fighting for breath,

128

fighting against blackness, against faintness, against death. If she could get the revolver, but she could not. She could not even gasp for breath, for there were iron hands upon her throat. She twisted and thrust and got free and had a great gasp of air and tried to scream, and then hands were there again, choking the scream.

She kept pulling at those hands – pulling at something – pulling – but it was easy to drop into that encircling blackness – easy to become part of it – part of it. . . .

Somewhere, somehow, in some curious, dim nether world very much time had passed. And someone was insisting that she return, forcing her to come back, making her open her eyes and listen and leave that dizzy place of blackness.

'She's opened her eyes,' cried a voice with a curious break in it. Susan stirred, became curious, opened her eyes again, saw a confused circle of faces bending over her, remembered, and screamed:

'Let me go . . . *let me go*. . . .'

'It's all right – it's all right, Susan. Look at me. See, I'm Jim. You are all right. Look at me.'

She opened her eyes again and knew that Jim was there, and Lieutenant Mohrn and a great many other people. And she knew she was being wrapped in the eiderdown, and that Lieutenant Mohrn and Jim made a sort of a chair with their arms and carried her out of the room and down the stairs. And then all at once she was in Jim's car, warm and snug.

'I'll get the story from her when she's better,' said Jim shortly to Lieutenant Mohrn, who stood at the side of the car. Susan, in a very luxury of tears, was crying her heart out.

Jim let her cry and drove very swiftly. His profile looked remarkably grim. He said nothing even when they reached Susan's house, beyond ordering Huldah to prepare some hot milk.

The story of the Easter image ended as, for Susan, it had begun, in her own small library with a fire blazing cheerfully and the dog at her feet.

'What happened?' she said abruptly.

'Don't talk.'

'But I must talk.'

He looked at her.

'All right,' he said. 'But don't talk too much. We got in at the window. Saw the open window on the upper porch and heard – sounds. Got there just in time.' He looked back at the fire and was suddenly very grim again.

'Where is – *she?*' whispered Susan.

'Where she belongs. Look here, if you must

130

talk, Sue, how did you know it was that woman? She confessed; had to. She had the gun, you know. The one that killed the butler.'

'It couldn't be anyone else,' Susan said slowly. 'But there wasn't any evidence.'

'Huh?' said Jim, in a startled manner.

'I mean,' said Susan hurriedly, 'there was only my own feeling, the things I saw and heard and felt about the people involved. It was all intangible, you see, until I put the things I knew on paper – chronologically, as they revealed themselves. Then all at once there was a tangible answer. But there weren't ever any direct material clues. Except the gun, there at the last. And the attack upon Felicia.'

A paper rustled in Jim's hand.

'Are those my notes?' asked Susan interestedly.

'Yes – Lieutenant Mohrn wanted you to explain them –'

'Very well,' she said. 'But it's rather like a – a –'

'Problem in algebra,' suggested Jim, smiling.

'No,' said Susan hastily. She had never been happy with algebraic terms. 'It was more like a – patchwork quilt. Just small unrelated scraps, you know, and a great many of them. And then you put them together in the only way they'll all fit, and there you have a pattern.'

Jim read:

' "*Noise in the night that must have been crash of Venetian glass and someone brushed my door; thus person breaking glass probably one of household.*" What on earth is that?'

'Part of the campaign against Felicia,' said Susan. 'It was evident from the first that there was a deliberate and very cruel campaign in progress against Felicia. The glass broken, her flowers dying always – William had said, she told me, something about acid in the water – her kitten, the knitting – it was all part of the plot. Go on.'

' "*Why is Felicia the focus of attack?*" Obviously someone wanted her either to do something that she had to be forced to do, or wanted her out of the way entirely.'

'Both,' said Susan and shivered.

' "*Gladstone has a roving eye*" '

'Kisses maids,' said Susan. 'Kisses anything feminine in a uniform.'

'Did he –' said Jim, threatening.

'Slightly,' said Susan, and added hurriedly; 'The whole thing, though, was centred about the Easter devil.'

'The *what!*' said Jim.

She told him, then, the whole story.

132

'So you see,' she said finally. 'It seemed to me that this was the situation. Mrs. Denisty ruled the household, controlled the purse strings, and was against divorce. Someone was deliberately playing on Felicia's nerves by threatening her with the Easter devil and by contriving all sorts of subtle ways of persecution. In this campaign the murder of the butler began to look like nothing more than an incident, for evidently the campaign was continuing. Then, when I found that the bridge had been tampered with – you can see for yourself to-morrow – there's a place where it is quite evident; the nails holding the planks there in the middle have been taken out and then replaced. It would have been a very bad fall, for it's just over the deepest part of the ravine – and I realized that owing to the French lessons Felicia would have been the first to cross the bridge in the morning, was, in fact, the only one in the household who crossed it daily and at a regular time. I knew thus that the campaign against Felicia had already reached its climax once, and yet had been, for some reason, interrupted.'

'Then you think that William was murdered because he saw too much?'

'And because he would have told. And his necessary murder, of course, delayed the plot against Felicia. Delayed it until the murderer realized that it could be used as a tool.'

'Tool?'

'A reason for what was to appear to be Felicia's suicide.'

Jim looked at the paper and read: ' *"Dorothy inquires about William; Dorothy seems sincere only when she talks of Mother Denisty ruling the house. Why? Dorothy hints that Mother Denisty knows something of William's murder. Why? Is this smoke-screen or sheer hatred of Mrs. Denisty? Dorothy nervous and quick-spoken until I lead her to spot where William was killed; is then poised and calm. Dorothy hints at Felicia becoming suicidal. Why?"* '

'Exactly,' said Susan. 'Why, if not because she's keenly interested in the police inquiry – because she resents Mrs. Denisty's influence, and thus in some way Mrs. Denisty must have opposed Dorothy's own purposes – because she knows too much of the murder herself to permit herself to be anything but extremely guarded and careful in speech and manner when the subject is brought up. When you add up everything, there's just one answer. Just one pattern in which everything fits. and the knitting brought Dorothy directly into it again; that is, none of the family could have pulled out the knitting, the image didn't do it. I felt sure Felicia hadn't, and that left only Dorothy who was free to come and go in the house. But Gladstone pretended publicly that he wasn't afraid of the image, and told Felicia privately that he *was* afraid of it. Believed in its power for evil. You see, Gladstone had to make an issue of something. So he chose the Easter image. It was at the same time a point of disagreement between him and Felicia and a medium through which to work upon Felicia – it's nothing but a painted piece of wood – but I don't like it myself,' said Susan. 'He couldn't have chosen a better tool. But it was Dorothy who murdered and was ready to murder again.'

'Then Gladstone –'

'Gladstone wanted a divorce, but wanted to drive Felicia to ask for it herself, owing to his mother's feeling about divorce. Dorothy had to be in the conspiracy, for she was strongly and directly concerned. But there was this difference: Gladstone – who must have thought he had hit on an exceedingly ingenious plan – only wanted to induce Felicia to leave him. *But Dorothy had other plans.* It wasn't fear that Felicia saw in her eyes: it was hate. I knew that when she talked to me of Felicia's possible suicide. There was the strangest impression that she was paving the way, so to speak; it was then that I realized

Felicia's danger. Yet I had no proof. It was, as I said, altogether intangible. Nothing definite. Except, of course, the bridge. If I'd had only one real, material clue I shouldn't have worried so. The footsteps on the bridge, though, were a help, because then I had a link between Dorothy and Gladstone, and I hadn't had that – except intangibly – up till then. But I also realized then that he must have told Dorothy the things Felicia had said to me, that Dorothy would realize that it was dangerous to permit Felicia to talk and that Dorothy would probably act at once. Would carry out the plan that had once been interrupted.'

'But you were not sure of this. You had no proof.'

'Proof?' said Susan. 'Why, no, there was no proof. And no evidence. But I would not have dared deny the evidence of my – intangibles.'

Jim grinned rather apologetically at her. 'After all,' he said. 'There's plenty of proof now. They think Dorothy intended to kill Felicia and leave the gun with Felicia's finger prints on it, thus indicating suicide and also that Felicia had shot the butler herself – hence her possession of the gun, hence also the suicide. Remorse. Of course, there were a hundred ways for Dorothy to have secured the gun.'

136

He paused and looked thoughtfully and soberly into the fire.

'Intangibles,' he said presently. 'But not so darned intangible after all. But all the same, young woman, you are going to get the worst scolding you ever had in all your life. The *chance* you took –' He stopped abruptly and looked away from Susan, and Susan smoothed back her hair.

'Yes,' she said in a small voice. 'But I've got to go back there.'

'Go back!' cried Jim Byrne explosively. 'There?'

'Yes, I forgot to burn the Easter image,' said Susan Dare.

The dog grunted and stretched. The fire was warm, the house at peace, the woman at home where she ought to be, and she hadn't seen the scratch on his nose after all.

ETHEL LINA WHITE

Ann Shelley, M.A. in
The Gilded Pupil

The essential part of this tale is that Ann Shelley was an Oxford M.A.

Unfortunately, so many other young women had the same idea of going to College and getting a degree, that she found it difficult to harness her qualifications with a job. Therefore she considered herself lucky when she was engaged as resident governess to Stella Williams, aged fifteen – the only child of a millionaire manufacturer.

It was not until her final interview with Stella's mother, in a sunroom which was a smother of luxury, that she understood the exact nature of her duties. Lady Williams – a beautiful porcelain person, with the brains of a butterfly – looked at her with appealing violet eyes.

'It's so difficult to explain, Miss Shelly. Of course, my husband considers education comes first, but what *I* want is someone to exercise a moral influence on Stella. She – she's not normal.'

'Thymus gland?' hinted Ann.

'Oh, far worse. She won't wash.'

Ann thought of the times she had been sent upstairs to remove a water-mark, because she had overslept, or wanted to finish a thriller; and she began to laugh.

'That's normal, at her age,' she explained. 'Schoolgirls often scamp washing.'

Lady Williams looked sceptical, but relieved.

'The trouble began,' she said, 'when she was too old for a nurse. Nannie used to wash and dress her, like a baby. But she refuses to let her maid do anything but impersonal things, like clothes. It's her idea of independence. She's terribly clever and Socialistic. She'll try to catch you out.'

'That sounds stimulating,' smiled Ann.

All the same, she was not impressed pleasantly by her new pupil. Stella was unattractive, aggressive, and superior. Her sole recommendation to Ann's favour was her intelligence, which was far above the average.

On her first Saturday half-holiday, Ann walked out to the grounds of Arlington Manor – the residence of the Earl of Blankshire – to visit her old governess, Miss West. It was a

139

May day of exciting weather, with concealed lighting bursting through a white windy sky. She thrilled with a sense of liberation, when she turned to the road through the woods, where the opening beeches were an emerald filigree against the blue shadows of the undergrowth.

Miss West's cottage suggested a fairy-tale, with its thatched roof and diamond-paned windows. It stood in a clearing, and was surrounded by a small garden, then purple with clumps of irises.

Ann's knock was answered by the maid, Maggie – a strapping country girl. She showed the visitor into the bed-sitting-room, where her mistress, who was crippled with rheumatism, was sitting up in bed.

Miss West was an old woman, for she had also been governess to Ann's mother. Her mouth and chin had assumed the nutcracker of age, so that she looked rather like an old witch, with her black blazing eyes and snowy hair.

Her dominant quality was her vitality. Ann could still feel it playing on her, like a battery, as they exchanged greetings.

'I love your little house,' she remarked later, when Maggie had brought in tea. 'But it's very lonely. Are you ever nervous?'

'Nervous of what?' asked Miss West.

'There's nothing here to steal, and no money. Everyone knows that the Earl is my banker.'

This was her way of explaining that she was a penniless pensioner of the Earl, whom she had taught in his nursery days.

'Every morning, someone comes down from the Manor, with the day's supplies,' she said. 'At night, a responsible person visits me for my orders and complaints.... Oh, you needn't look down your nose. The Earl is in *my* debt. He is prolonging my life at a trifling expense to himself; but I saved his life, when he was a child, at the risk of my own.'

Her deep voice throbbed as she added, 'I still feel there is nothing so precious as Life.'

Later, in that small bewitched room, Ann was to remember her words.

'Life's big things appeal most to me,' she confessed. 'Oxford was wonderful – every minute of it. And I'm just living for my marriage with Kenneth. I told you I was engaged. He's a doctor on a ship, and we'll have to wait. In between, I'm just marking time.'

'You have the important job of moulding character,' Miss West reminded her. 'How does your gilded pupil progress?'

'She's a gilded pill.' Ann grimaced. 'A gilded pupil.'

'Is Oxford responsible for your idea of

humour?' asked Miss West, who had a grudge against a University education.

'No, it's the result of living in a millionaire's family. Please, may I come to see you, every Saturday afternoon? You make me feel re-charged.'

Although Miss West had acted like a mental tonic, Ann was conscious of a period of stagnation, when she walked back through the wood. She taught, in order to live, and went to see an old woman, as recreation. Life was dull.

It might not have appeared so flat, had she known that she was marked down already for a leading part in a sinister drama, and that she had been followed all the way to the cottage.

For the next few weeks life continued to be monotonous for Ann, but it grew exciting for Stella, as, gradually, she felt the pull of her governess' attraction. Ann had a charming appearance and definite personality. She made no attempt to rouse her pupil's personal pride by shock-tactics, but relied on the contrast between her own manicured hands and the girl's neglected nails.

Presently she was able to report progress to the young ship's doctor.

'My three years at Oxford have not been

wasted,' she wrote. 'The Gilded Pupill has begun to wash.'

In her turn she became fonder of Stella, especially when she discovered that the girl's aggressive manner was a screen for an inferiority-complex.

'I always feel people hate me,' she confided to her governess one day. 'I'm ashamed of having a millionaire father. *He* didn't make his money. Others make it for him. He ought to pay them a real spending-income, and, automatically, increase the demand, and create fresh employment.'

Ann found these Socialistic debates rather a trial of tact, but she enjoyed the hours of study. Stella was a genuine student, and always read up her subject beforehand, so that lessons took somewhat the form of discussions and explanations. Ann was spared the drudgery of correcting French exercises and problems in Algebra.

But her gain was someone else's loss. She had no idea how seriously she was restricting the activities of another character in the Plot.

Doris – the schoolroom maid – searched daily amid the fragments in the wastepaper-basket for something which she had been ordered to procure. And she searched in vain.

When Stella's devotion to the bathroom was deepening to passion, she began to grow jealous of her governess' private hours.

'Do you go to the Pictures on Saturday?' she asked.

'No. I visit an old witch in a cottage in the wood.'

'Take me with you.'

'You'd be bored. It's my old governess.'

'*Your* governess? I'd love to see her. *Please.*'

Ann had to promise a vague 'some day'. Although she was sorry to disappoint Stella, she could not allow her to encroach on her precious liberty.

By this time, however, her time-table was an established fact to the brains of the Plot. Therefore, the next Saturday she visited Miss West she was followed by a new trailer.

She noticed him when she came out of the great gates of the millionaire's mansion, because he aroused a momentary sense of repugnance. He was fair and rather womanish in appearance, but his good looks were marred by a cruel red triangular mouth.

He kept pace with her on the opposite side of the street, when she was going through the town, but she shook him off later on. Therefore it gave her quite a shock when she turned into the beech-avenue – now a green

144

tunnel – to hear his footsteps a little distance in the rear.

Although she was furious with herself, she hurried to reach the cottage, which was quite close. The door was opened before she could knock, because her arrival was the signal for Maggie's release. It was Ann herself who had suggested the extra leisure for the maid while she kept the old lady company.

Miss West, whose bed faced the window, greeted her with a question.

'When did you lose your admirer?'

'Who?' asked Ann, in surprise.

'I refer to the weedy boy who always slouches past the minute after your knock.'

'I've never noticed him. . . . But I thought I was followed here to-day by a specially unpleasant-looking man.'

'Hum. We'd better assume that you were. . . . How much money have you in your bag?'

'More than I care to lose.'

'Then leave all the notes with me. I'll get the Manor folk to return them to you by registered post. . . . And remember, if the man attacks you on your way home, don't resist. Give him your bag – and run.'

'You're arranging a cheerful programme for me,' laughed Ann.

She might not have felt so amused had she

known that the whole time she was inside the cottage the man was not far away, crouched behind a belt of rhododendrons. Inside a deep pocket of his full belted coat was coiled something like a gigantic black slug.

It was a stocking stuffed with sand.

When nine struck, Miss West told her to go.

'Maggie is due now, any minute,' she told her, 'and so is the housekeeper from the Manor. Good-bye – and don't forget it means "God be with you".'

Ann was not nervous, but when she walked down the garden path she could not help contrasting the dark green twilight of the woods with the sun-splashed beech avenue of the afternoon. Clumps of foxgloves glimmered whitely through the gloom, and in the distance an owl hooted to his mate.

She passed close by the bushes where the man was hiding. He could have touched her had he put out his hand. She was his quarry, whom he had followed to the cottage, so he looked at her intently.

Her expensive bag promised a rich haul. Yet he let her go by, and waited, instead, for someone who was of only incidental interest to the Plot.

A few minutes later Maggie charged down the avenue like a young elephant, for she was

146

late. She had not a nerve in her body, and only threepence in her purse. As she passed the rhododendron thicket, a shadow slipped out of it like an adder – a black object whirled round in the air – and Maggie fell down on the ground like a log.

The mystery attack was a nine-days' wonder, for bag-snatching was unknown in the district. But while Maggie was recovering from slight concussion in hospital, Ann had the unpleasant task of mentally bludgeoning her pupil out of a 'rave'. After the weekly visit of the hairdresser, Stella appeared in the school-room with her hair cut and waved in the same fashion as Ann's.

'Like it?' she asked self-consciously.

'It's charming.' Ann had to be tender with the inferiority-complex. 'But I liked your old style better. That was *you*. Don't copy me, Stella. I should never forgive myself if I robbed you of your individuality.'

Stella wilted like a pimpernel in wet weather.

'I'm not going to have a crush on you,' she declared. 'Too definitely feeble. But we're friends, aren't we? Let's have a sort of Friend's Charter, with a secret signature, when we write to each other. Like this.' She scrawled a five-fingered star on a piece of paper and explained it eagerly. 'My name.'

Ann was aware that Doris, the school-room maid, was listening with a half-grin, and she decided to nip the nonsense in the bud.

'You'll want a Secret Society next, you baby,' she said, as she crumpled up the paper. 'Now, suppose we call it a day and go to the Pictures.'

Stella especially enjoyed that afternoon's entertainment, because the film was about a kidnapped girl, and she was excited by the personal implication. 'If a kidnapper ever got me, I'd say 'Good luck' to him. He'd deserve it,' she boasted as they drove home. 'They wouldn't decoy me into a taxi with a fake message.'

Ann's private feeling was that Stella's intelligence was not likely to be tested, since she ran no possible risk. Lady Williams was nervous on the score of her valuable jewellery, so the house was burglar-proof, with flood-lit grounds and every kind of electric alarm.

Besides this, Stella either went out in the car, driven by a trusted chauffeur, or took her walks with a positive pack of large dogs.

So it was rather a shock to Ann when the girl lowered her voice.

'I'll tell you a secret. They've had a shot for me. They sent one of our own cars to the dancing class; but I noticed Hereford wasn't driving, so I wouldn't get in. I wouldn't tell them at home because of Mother. She's beautiful and sweet, but she'd go to a Queen's Hall Concert expecting a Walt Disney Silly Symphony.'

Ann, who was still under the influence of the Picture, was horrified.

'Stella,' she cried. 'I want you to promise me something. If ever you get a note, signed by me, *take no notice of it.*'

'I promise. But if you signed it with our star, I'd *know* it was genuine. And if you were in danger, nothing and no-one would stop me from coming to your rescue.'

'Single-handed, like the screen heroines, who blunder into every trap?'

'Not me. I'll bring the police with me. . . . Isn't that our school-room maid coming down the drive? Isn't she gorgeous?'

Doris, transformed by a Marina cap and generous lip-stick, minced past the car. She had to be smart, because she was meeting a fashionable gentleman with a cruel red mouth.

When she saw him in the distance, she anticipated his question by shaking her head.

'No good swearing at me,' she told him. 'I can't get what isn't there. But I've brought you something else.'

149

She gave him a sheet of crumpled paper on which was the rough drawing of a star.

The next time Ann went to the cottage in the wood the door was opened by the new maid – an ice-cold competent brunette in immaculate livery. There was no doubt she was a domestic treasure and a great improvement on Maggie; but Ann was repelled by the expression of her thin-lipped mouth.

'I don't like your new maid's face,' she said to her old governess when Coles had carried out the tea-table.

'Neither do I,' remarked Miss West calmly. 'She's far too good for my situation – yet she's no fool. My opinion is she's wanted by the police and has come here to hide. It's an ideal spot.'

'But you won't keep her?'

'Why not? She's an excellent maid. There's no reason why I should not benefit by the special circumstances, if any. After all it's only my suspicion.'

'What about her references?'

'Superlative. Probably forged. The house-keeper hadn't time to enquire too closely. The place isn't popular after the attack on Maggie.'

'But I don't like to think of you alone at her mercy.'

'Don't worry about me. She's been to the cupboard and found out it's bare. I've nothing to lose.'

Ann realized the sense of Miss West's argument, especially as she was in constant touch with the Manor. Not long afterwards she wondered whether she had misjudged the woman, for she received a letter by the next morning's post which indicated that she was not altogether callous.

Its address was the cottage in the wood.

'Dear Madam,' it ran. 'Pardon the liberty of my writing to you, but I feel responsible for Miss West in case anything happens sudden to her and there's an Inquest. I would be obliged if you would tell me is her heart bad and what to do in case of a sudden attack. I don't like to trouble her ladyship as I am a stranger to her and Miss West bites my head off if I ask her. I could not ask you today because she is suspicious of whispering. Will you kindly drop me a line in return and oblige, Yours respectfully, Marion Coles.'

Ann hastily wrote the maid a brief note saying that Miss West had good health – apart from the crippling rheumatism – but recommending a bottle of brandy in case of emergency. She posted it, and forgot the matter.

Meanwhile, Miss West was finding Coles' competency a pleasant change after Maggie's slipshod methods. On the following Saturday, when she carried in her mistress' lunch, Miss West looked, with approval, at her spotless apron and muslin collar.

After she had finished her well-cooked cutlet and custard, she lay back and closed her eyes in order to be fresh for Ann's visit. The cottage was very peaceful with a flicker of green shade outside the window; there was none of the noisy clatter from the kitchen which used to advertise the fact when Maggie washed up — only the ticking of the grandfather's clock and the cooing of wood-pigeons.

She had begun to doze when she heard the opening of the front door. Her visitor was before her usual time.

'Ann,' she called.

Instead of her old pupil, a strange woman entered the bedroom. Her fashionably thin figure was defined by a tight black suit, and a halo hat revealed a sharp rouged face.

As Miss West stared at her, she gave a cry of recognition.

'*Coles.*'

The woman sneered at her like a camel.

'Here's two gentlemen come to see you,' she announced.

As she spoke, two men, dressed with flashy smartness, sauntered into the room. One was blond and handsome except for a red triangular mouth; the other had the small cunning eyes and low-set ears of an elementary criminal type.

'Go out of my room,' ordered Miss West. 'Coles, you are discharged.'

The men only laughed as they advanced to the bed.

'We're only going to make you safer, old lady,' said the fair man. 'You might fall out of bed and hurt yourself. See?'

Miss West did not condescend to struggle while her feet and hands were secured with cords. Her wits told her that she would need to conserve every ounce of strength.

'Aren't you taking an unnecessary precaution with a bedridden woman?' she asked scornfully.

'Nothing too good for you, sweetheart,' the fair man told her.

'Why have you come here? My former maid has told you that there is nothing of value in my cottage.'

'Nothing but you, Beautiful.'

'How dare you be insolent to me? Take off your hats in a lady's presence.'

The men only laughed. They sat and smoked cigarettes in silence until a knock

153

on the front door made them spring to their feet.

'Let her in,' ordered the ringleader.

Miss West strained at her cords as Coles went out of the room. Her black eyes glared with helpless fury when Ann entered and stood – horror-stricken – in the doorway.

'Don't *dare* touch her,' she cried.

The men merely laughed again as they seized the struggling girl, forced her down on a bedroom chair, and began to bind her ankles.

'Ann,' commanded the old governess. 'Keep still. They're three to one. An elementary knowledge of arithmetic should tell you resistance is useless. But I forgot. You were finished at Oxford.'

The pedantic old voice steadied Ann's nerves.

'Are *you* all right, Miss West?' she asked coolly.

'Quite comfortable, thanks.'

'Good.' Ann turned to the men. 'What do you want?'

They did not answer, but nodded to Coles, who placed a small table before Ann. With the deft movements of a well-trained maid, she arranged stationery – stamped with Miss West's address – and writing materials.

Then the fair man explained the situation.

'The Williams kid wot you teach is always pestering you to come here and see the old lady. Now, you're going to write her a nice little note inviting her to tea this afternoon.'

Ann's heart hammered as she realized that she had walked into a trap. The very simplicity of the scheme was its safeguard. She was the decoy-bird. The kidnappers had only to instal a spy in the Williams' household to study the habits of the governess.

Unfortunately she had led them to an ideal rendezvous – the cottage in the wood.

'*No,*' she said.

The next second she shivered as something cold was pressed to her temple.

'We'll give you five minutes to make up your mind,' said the fair man, glancing at the grandfather's clock. 'Then, we shoot.'

Ann gritted her teeth. In that moment her reason told her that she was probably acting from false sentiment and a confused set of values. But logic was of no avail. Like the intellectual youth of the Nation, who went over the top while probably cursing the insanity of War, she knew she had to sacrifice herself for an Ideal.

She could not betray her trust.

'No,' she said again.

The second man crossed to the bed and pressed his revolver to Miss West's head.

'Her too,' he said.

Ann looked at her old governess, in an agony, imploring her forgiveness.

'She's only fifteen,' she said piteously, as though in excuse.

'And I'm an old woman,' grunted Miss West. 'Your reasoning is sound. But you forget someone younger than your pupil. Your unborn son.'

Ann's face quivered, but she shook her head. Then the old governess spoke with the rasp of authority in her voice.

'Ann, I'm ashamed of you. What is money compared with two valuable lives, not to mention those still to come? I understand these – gentlemen – do not wish to injure your pupil. They only want to collect a ransom.'

'That's right, lady,' agreed the fair man. 'We won't do her no harm. This will tell the old man all he'll want to know.'

He laid down a typewritten demand note on the table and added a direction to Ann.

'When we've gone off with the kid, nip off to the old man as fast as you can and give him this.'

'With her legs tied to a chair?' asked the

156

deep sarcastic voice of the old woman.

'She got her hands free, ain't she? Them knots will take some undoing, but it's up to her, ain't it?'

'True. No doubt she will manage to free herself.... But suppose she writes this note and the young lady does not accept the invitation? What then?'

The fair man winked at his companion.

'Then you'll both be unlucky,' he replied.

Ann listened in dull misery. She could not understand the drift of Miss West's questions. They only prolonged the agony. Both of them knew they could place no reliance on the promises of the kidnappers. The men looked a pair of merciless beasts.

If she wrote that note, she would lure her poor little gilded pupill to her death.

She started as her governess spoke sharply to her.

'*Ann*, you've heard what these gentlemen have said.' She added in bitter mockery of their speech, '*Gentlemen* what keeps their hats on in the presence of ladies, wouldn't never break their word. *Write that note.*'

Ann could not believe her ears. Yet she could feel the whole force of her vitality playing on her like an electric battery. It reminded her of a former experience when she was a child. Her uncle, who paid for her education, was an Oxford don, and he raised an objection against Miss West because she was unqualified.

In the end he consented to give his niece a viva-voce examination, on the result of which depended the governess' fate.

Ann passed the test triumphantly, but she always felt, privately, that Miss West supplied the right answers as she sat staring at her pupil with hypnotic black eyes.

Now she knew that the old magic was at work again. Miss West was trying to tell her something without the aid of words.

Suddenly the knowledge came. Her old governess was playing for time. Probably she was expecting some male visitors from the Manor, as the Earl and his sons often came to the cottage. What she, herself, had to do was to stave off the five-minute sentence of death by writing a note to Stella which was hallmarked as a forgery, so that the girl would not come.

As she hesitated she remembered that she had extracted a promise from her pupil to disregard any message. The question was, whether it would be obeyed, for she knew the strength of her fatal attraction and that Stella was eager to visit the cottage.

Hoping for the best, she began to write, disguising her handwriting by a backward slant.

'Dear Stella' –

With an oath the man snatched up the paper and threw it on the floor in a crumpled ball.

'None of them monkey tricks,' he snarled. 'We know your proper writing. And sign it with *this*.'

Ann's hope died as the man produced the letter which she had written to Coles about Miss West's health, and also Stella's rough drawing of a star. She was defeated by the evidence – a specimen of her handwriting – for which Doris the school-room maid had searched in vain – and the secret signature.

'I – can't,' she said, feebly pushing away the paper.

Again the pistol was pressed to her head.

'Don't waste no time,' growled the fair man.

'Don't waste no time,' echoed Miss West. 'Ann, *write*.'

There was a spark in the old woman's eyes and the flash of Wireless. Impelled to take up the pen, Ann wrote quickly in a firm hand, and signed her note with a faithful copy of the star.

The men hung over her, watching every stroke, and comparing the writing with Coles' letter.

'Don't put no dots,' snarled the fair man, who plainly suspected a cypher when Ann inserted a period.

He read the note again when it was finished, and then passed it to his companion, who pointed to a word suspiciously. The old woman and the girl looked at each other in an agony of suspense as they waited for the blow to fall.

Then the fair man turned sharply to Miss West.

'Spell "genwin", he commanded.

As she reeled off the correct spelling, he glanced doubtfully at his companion, who nodded.

'O.K.,' he said.

Miss West's grim face did not relax, and Ann guessed the reason. She was nerving herself for the second ordeal of Coles' inspection.

Fortunately, however, the men did not want their female confederate's opinion. The job was done and they wanted to rush it forward to its next stage. The fair man sealed the note and whistled on his fingers.

Instantly the weedy youth who had followed Ann to the cottage appeared from behind a clump of laurels in the drive, wheeling a bicycle. He snatched the letter from Coles and scorched away round the bend of the road.

Ann slumped back in her chair, feeling unstrung in every fibre. Nothing remained but to wait – wait – and pray Stella would not come.

The time seemed to pass very slowly inside the room. The men smoked in silence until the carpet was littered with cigarette stubs and the air veined with smoke. Miss West watched the clock as though she would galvanize the crawling minute-hand.

'Don't come,' agonized Ann. 'Stella, *don't come.*'

But absent treatment proved a failure, for Coles, who was hiding behind a curtain, gave a sudden hoot of triumph.

'The car's come.'

'Push the girl to the front,' commanded the fair man.

He helped to lift Ann's chair to the window, so that she saw the Williams' Lanchester waiting in front of the cottage. Stella stood on the drive, and the chauffeur, Hereford, was in the act of shutting the door. He sprang back to his seat, backed, saluted, and drove swiftly away.

Ann watched the car disappear with despairing eyes. She could not scream, because fingers were gripping her windpipe, nearly choking her. But Stella could distinguish the pale-blue blur of her frock behind the diamond-paned window, and she waved her hand as she ran eagerly up the garden path.

Had Ann been normal, she might have guessed the truth from Stella's reaction to the scene when she burst into the room. Instead of appearing surprised, she dashed to Ann and threw her arms around her.

'They didn't fool *me*,' she whispered.

Then she began to fight like a boxing-kangaroo in order to create the necessary distraction, while the police-car came round the bend of the drive.

The prelude to a successful raid was the millionaire's call for prompt action when his daughter brought him Ann's note.

'It's her writing and our private star,' she told him. 'But – read it.' He glanced at the few lines and laughed.

'An impudent forgery,' he said.

'No, it's an S.O.S. It looks like a second try for me.'

After she had told her father about the first unsuccessful attempt to kidnap her, he

162

realized the importance of nipping the gang's activities in the bud.

This seems the place to print the note which was the alleged composition of an Oxford M.A.

'Dear Stella, Miss West will be pleased if you will come to tea this afternoon. Don't waste no time, and don't run no risks. Let Hereford drive you in the car. To prove this is genuine, I'm signing it with our star, same as you done, one day in the school-room.

Yours, Ann Shelley, M.A.'

DOROTHY L SAYERS

Susan Tabbit in
Scrawns

The gate, on whose peeled and faded surface the name SCRAWNS was just legible in the dim light, fell to with a clap that shook the rotten gatepost and scattered a shower of drops from the drenched laurels. Susan Tabbit set down the heavy suitcase which had made her arm ache, and peered through the drizzle toward the little house.

It was a curious, lopsided, hunch-shouldered building, seeming not so much to preside over its patch of wintry garden as to be eavesdropping behind its own hedges. Against a streak of watery light in the west, its chimneystacks – one at either end – suggested pricked ears, intensely aware; the more so, that its face was blind.

Susan shivered a little, and thought regretfully of the cheerful bus that she had left at the bottom of the hill. The conductor had seemed just as much surprised as the station porter had been when she mentioned her destination. He had opened his mouth as though about to make some comment, but had thought better of it. She wished she had had the courage to ask him what sort of place she was coming to. Scrawns. It was a queer name; she had thought so when she had first seen it on Mrs. Wispell's notepaper. Susan Tabbit, care of Mrs. Wispell, Scrawns, Roman Way, Dedcaster.

Her married sister had pursed up her lips when Susan gave her the address, reading it aloud with an air of disapproval. 'What's she like, this Mrs. Wispell of Scrawns?' Susan had to confess that she did not know; she had taken the situation without an interview.

Now the house faced her, aloof, indifferent, but on the watch. No house should look so. She had been a fool to come; but it had been so evident that her sister was anxious to get her out of the house. There was no room for her, with all her brother-in-law's family coming. And she was short of money. She had thought it might be pleasant at Scrawns. House-parlormaid, to work with married couple; that had sounded all right. Three in the family; that was all right, to. In her last job there had been only herself and eight in family; she had looked forward to a light place and a lively kitchen.

'And what am I thinking about?' said

165

Susan, picking up the suitcase. 'The family'll be out, as like as not, at a party or something of that. There'll be a light in the kitchen all right, I'll be bound.'

She plodded over the sodden gravel, between two squares of lawn, flanked by empty beds and backed by a huddle of shrubbery; then turned along a path to the right, following the front of the house with its blank unwelcoming windows. The sidewalk was as dark as the front. She made out the outline of a french window, opening upon the path and, to her right, a wide herbaceous border, where tin labels, attached to canes, flapped forlornly. Beyond this there seemed to be a lawn, but the tall trees which surrounded it on all three sides drowned it in blackness and made its shape and extent a mystery. The path led on, through a half-open door that creaked as she pushed it back, and she found herself in a small, paved courtyard, across which the light streamed in a narrow beam from a small, lighted window.

She tried to look in at this window, but a net curtain veiled its lower half. She could only see the ceiling, low, with black rafters from one of which there hung a paraffin lamp. Passing the window she found a door and knocked.

With the first fall of the old-fashioned iron

knocker, a dog began to bark, loudly, incessantly, and furiously. She waited, her heart hammering, but nobody came. After a while she summoned up resolution to knock afresh. This time she thought she could distinguish, through the clamor, a movement within. The barking ceased, she heard a key turn and bolts withdrawn, and the door opened.

The light within came from a doorway on the left, and outlined against it, she was only aware of an enormous bulk and a dim triangle of whiteness, blocking her entrance to the house.

'Who is it?'

The voice was unlike any she had ever heard; curiously harsh and husky and sexless, like the voice of something strangled.

'My name's Tabbit – Susan Tabbit.'

'Oh, you're the new girl!' There was a pause, as though the speaker were trying, in the uncertain dusk, to sum her up and reckon out her possibilities.

'Come in.'

The looming bulk retreated, and Susan again lifted her suitcase and carried it inside.

'Mrs. Wispell got my letter, saying I was coming?'

'Yes; she got it. But one can't be too careful. It's a lonely place. You can leave your bag for Jarrock. This way.'

167

Susan stepped into the kitchen. It was a low room, not very large but appearing larger than it was because of the shadows thrown into the far corners by the wide shade of the hanging lamp. There was a good fire, which Susan was glad to see, and over the mantelpiece an array of polished copper pans winked reassuringly. Behind her she again heard the jarring of shot bolts and turned key. Then her jailer – why did that word leap uncalled into her mind? – came back and stepped for the first time into the light.

As before, her first overwhelming impression was of enormous height and size. The flat, white, wide face, the billowing breasts, the enormous girth of white-aproned haunch seemed to fill the room and swim above her. Then she forgot everything else in the shock of realizing that the huge woman was cross-eyed.

It was no mere cast; not even an ordinary squint. The left eye was swiveled so horribly far inward that half the iris was invisible, giving to that side of the face a look of blind and cunning malignity. The other eye was bright and dark and small, and fixed itself acutely on Susan's face.

'I'm Mrs. Jarrock,' said the woman in her odd, hoarse voice.

It was incredible to Susan that any man

168

who was not blind and deaf should have married a woman so hideously disfigured and with such a raven croak. She said: 'How do you do?' and extended a reluctant hand, which Mrs. Jarrock's vast palm engulfed in a grasp unexpectedly hard and masculine.

'You'll like a cup of tea before you change,' said Mrs. Jarrock. 'You can wait at table, I suppose?'

'Oh, yes, I'm used to that.'

'Then you'd better begin tonight. Jarrock's got his hands full with Mr. Alistair. It's one of his bad days. We was both upstairs, that's why you had to wait.' She again glanced sharply at the girl, and the swivel eye rolled unpleasantly and uncontrollably in its socket. She turned and bent to lift the kettle from the range, and Susan could not rid herself of the notion that the left eye was still squinting at her from its ambush behind the cook's flat nose.

'Is it a good place?' asked Susan.

'It's all right,' said Mrs. Jarrock, 'for them as isn't nervous. *She* don't trouble herself much, but that's only to be expected, as things are, and *he's* quiet enough, if you don't cross him. Mr. Alistair won't trouble you, that's Jarrock's job. There's your tea. Help yourself to milk and sugar. I wonder if Jarrock —'

169

She broke off short; set down the teapot and stood with her large head cocked sideways, as though listening to something going on above. Then she moved hastily across the kitchen, with a lightness of step surprising in so unwieldy a woman, and disappeared into the darkness of the passage. Susan, listening anxiously, thought she could hear a sound like moaning and a movement of feet across the raftered ceiling. In a few minutes, Mrs. Jarrock came back, took the kettle from the fire and handed it out to some unseen person in the passage. A prolonged whispering followed, after which Mrs. Jarrock again returned and, without offering any comment, began to make buttered toast.

Susan ate without relish. She had been hungry when she left the bus, but the atmosphere of the house disconcerted her. She had just refused a second slice of toast when she became aware that a man had entered the kitchen.

He was a tall man and powerfully built, but he stood in the doorway as though suspicious or intimidated; she realized that he had probably been standing there for some time before she observed him. Mrs. Jarrock, seeing Susan's head turn and remain arrested, looked round also.

'Oh, there you are, Jarrock. Come and take your tea.'

The man moved then, skirting the wall with a curious, crablike movement, and so coming by reluctant degrees to the opposite side of the fire, where he stood, his head averted, shooting a glance at Susan from the corner of his eye.

'This here's Susan,' said Mrs. Jarrock. 'It's to be hoped she'll settle down and be comfortable with us. I'll be glad to have her to help with the work, *as you* know, with one thing and another.'

'We'll do our betht to make things eathy for her,' said the man. He lisped oddly and, though he held out his hand, he still kept his head half averted, like a cat that refuses to take notice. He retreated into an armchair, drawn rather far back from the hearth, and sat gazing into the fire. The dog which had barked when Susan knocked had followed him into the room, and now came over and sniffed at the girl's legs, uttering a menacing growl.

'Be quiet, Crippen,' said the man. 'Friends.'

The dog, a large brindled bull terrier, was apparently not reassured. He continued to growl, till Jarrock, hauling him back by the collar, gave him a smart cuff on the head

171

and ordered him under the table, where he went, sullenly. In bending to beat the dog, Jarrock for the first time turned his full face upon Susan, and she saw, with horror, that the left side of it, from the cheekbone downward, could scarcely be called a face, for it was seamed and puckered by a horrible scar, which had dragged the mouth upward into the appearance of a ghastly grin, while the left-hand side of the jaw seemed shapeless and boneless, a mere bag of wrinkled flesh.

Is everybody in this house maimed and abnormal? she thought, desperately. As though in answer to her thoughts, Mrs. Jarrock spoke to her husband.

'Has he settled down now?'

'Oh, he's quiet enough,' replied the man, lisping through his shattered teeth. 'He'll do all right.' He retired again to his corner and began sucking in his buttered toast, making awkward sounds.

'If you've finished your tea,' said Mrs. Jarrock, 'I'd better show you your room. Have you taken Susan's bag up, Jarrock?'

The man nodded without speaking, and Susan, in some trepidation, followed the huge woman, who had lit a candle in a brass candlestick.

'You'll find the stairs awkward at first,' said the hoarse voice, 'and you'll have to mind your head in these passages. Built in the year one, this place was, and by a crazy builder at that, if you ask me.'

She glided noiselessly along a narrow corridor and out into a square flagged hall, where a small oil lamp, heavily shaded, seemed to make darkness deeper; then mounted a flight of black oak stairs with twisted banisters of polished oak and shining oak treads, in which the candlelight was reflected on wavering yellow pools.

'There's only one staircase,' said Mrs. Jarrock. 'Unhandy, I calls it, but you'll have to do your best. You'll have to wait till he's shut himself up of a morning before you bring down the slops; he don't like to see pails about. This here's their bedroom and that's the spare and this is Mr. Alistair's room. Jarrock sleeps in with him, of course, in case –' She stopped at the door, listening; then led the way up a narrow attic staircase.

'You're in here. It's small, but you're by yourself. And I'm next door to you.'

The candle threw their shadows, gigantically distorted, upon the sloping ceiling, and Susan thought, fantastically: If I stay here, I shall grow the wrong shape, too.

'And the big attic's the master's place. You don't have nothing to do with that. Much as your place or ours is worth to poke your nose round the door. He keeps it locked, anyway.' The cook laughed, a hoarse, throaty chuckle. 'Queer things he keeps in there, I must say. I've seen 'em – when he brings 'em downstairs, that is. He's a funny one, is Mr. Wispell. Well, you'd better get changed into your black, then I'll take you to the mistress.'

Susan dressed hurriedly before the little heart-shaped mirror with its old, greenish glass that seemed to absorb more of the candlelight than it reflected. She pulled aside the check window curtain and looked out. It was almost night, but she contrived to make out that the attic looked over the garden at the side of the house. Beneath her lay the herbaceous border, and beyond that, the tall trees stood up like a wall. The room itself was comfortably furnished, though, as Mrs. Jarrock had said, extremely small and twisted into a curious shape by the slanting flue of the great chimney, which ran up on the left-hand side and made a great elbow beside the bed head. There was a minute fireplace cut into the chimney, but it had an unused look. Probably, thought Susan, it would smoke.

At the head of the stairs, she hesitated, candle in hand. She was divided between a dread of solitude and a dread of what she was to meet below. She tiptoed down the attic stair and emerged upon the landing. As

174

she did so, she saw the back of Jarrock flitting down the lower flight, and noticed that he had left the door of 'Mr. Alistair's' room open behind him. Urged by a curiosity powerful enough to overcome her uneasiness, she crept to the door and peeped in.

Facing her was an old-fashioned tester bed with dull green hangings; a shaded reading lamp burned beside it on a small table. The man on the bed lay flat on his back with closed eyes; his face was yellow and transparent as wax, with pinched, sharp nostrils; one hand, thin as a claw, lay passive upon the green counterpane; the other was hidden in the shadows of the curtain. Certainly, if Jarrock had been speaking of Mr. Alistair, he was right; this man was quiet enough now.

'Poor gentleman,' whispered Susan. 'He's passed away.' And while the words were still on her lips a great bellow of laughter burst forth from somewhere on the floor below. It was monstrous, gargantuan, fantastic; it was an outrage upon the silent house. Susan started back, and the snuffer, jerking from the candlestick, leaped into the air and went ringing and rolling down the oak staircase to land with a brazen clang on the flags below.

Somewhere a door burst open and a loud

175

voice, with a hint of that preposterous mirth still lurking in its depths, bawled out:

'What's that? What the devil's that? Jarrock! Did you make that filthy noise?'

'I beg your pardon, sir,' said Susan, advancing in some alarm to the stairhead. 'It was my fault, sir. I shook the candlestick and the snuffer fell down. I am very sorry, sir.'

'You?' said the man. 'Who the devil are you? Come down and let's have a look at you. Oh!' as Susan's black dress and muslin apron came into his view at the turn of the stair, 'the new housemaid, hey! That's a pretty way to announce yourself. A damned good beginning! Don't you do it again, that's all. I won't have noise, d'you understand? All the noise in this house is made by me. That's my prerogative, if you know what the word means. Hey? Do you understand?'

'Yes, sir. I won't let it happen again, sir.'

'That's right. And look here. If you've made a dent in those boards, d'you know what I'll do? Hey? I'll have the insides out of you, d'you hear?' He jerked back his big, bearded head, and his great guffaw seemed to shake the old house like a gust of wind. 'Come on, girl, I won't eat you this time. Let's see your face. Your legs are all right, anyway. I won't have a housemaid with thick legs. Come in here and be vetted. Sidonia, here's the new girl, chucking the furniture all over the place the minute she's in the house. Did you hear it? Did you ever hear anything like it? Hey? Ha, ha!'

He pushed Susan in front of him into a sitting room furnished in deep orange and rich blues and greens like a peacock's tail, and with white walls that caught and flung back the yellow lamplight. The windows were closely shuttered and barred.

On a couch drawn up near the fire a girl was lying. She had a little, white, heart-shaped face, framed and almost drowned in a mass of heavy red hair, and on her long fingers were several old and heavy rings. At her husband's boisterous entry she rose rather awkwardly and uncertainly.

'Walter, dear, don't shout so. My head aches, and you'll frighten the poor girl. So you're Susan. How are you? I hope you had a good journey. Are Mr. and Mrs. Jarrock looking after you?'

'Yes, thank you madam.'

'Oh! then that's all right.' She looked a little helplessly at her husband, and then back to Susan. 'I hope you'll be a good girl, Susan.'

'I shall try to give satisfaction, madam.'

'Yes, yes, I'm sure you will.' She laughed, on a high, silver note like a bird's call.

'Mrs. Jarrock will put you in the way of things. I hope you'll be happy and stay with us.' Her pretty, aimless laughter tinkled out again.

'I hope Susan won't disappear like the last one,' said Mr. Wispell. Susan caught a quick glance darted at him by his wife, but before she could decide whether it was one of fear or of warning, they were interrupted. A bell pealed sharply with a jangling of wires, and in the silence that followed the two Wispells stared uneasily at each other.

'What the devil's that?' said Mr. Wispell. 'I only hope to heaven –'

Jarrock came in. He held a telegram in his hand. Wispell snatched it from him and tore it open. With an exclamation of distaste and alarm he handed it to his wife, who uttered a sharp cry.

'Walter, we can't! She mustn't! Can't we stop her?'

'Don't be a fool, Sidonia. How can we stop her?'

'Yes, Walter. But don't you understand? She'll expect to find Helen here.'

'Oh, Lord!' said Mr. Wispell.

Susan went early to bed. Dinner had been a strained and melancholy meal. Mrs. Wispell talked embarrassed nothings at intervals: Mr.

Wispell seemed sunk in a savage gloom, from which he only roused himself to bark at Susan for more potatoes or another slice of bread. Nor were things much better in the kitchen, for it seemed that a visitor was expected.

'Motoring down from York,' muttered Mrs. Jarrock. 'Goodness knows when they'll get here. But that's her all over. No consideration, and never had. I'm sorry for the mistress, that's all.'

Jarrock's distorted mouth twisted into a still more ghastly semblance of a grin.

'Rich folks must have their way,' he said. 'Four years ago it was the same thing. A minute's notice and woe betide if everything's not right. But we'll be ready for her, oh! we'll be ready for her, you'll see.' He chuckled gently to himself.

Mrs. Jarrock gave a curious, sly smile. 'You'll have to help me with the spare room, Susan,' she said.

Later, coming down into the scullery to fill a hot-water bottle, Susan found the Jarrocks in close confabulation beside the sink.

'And see you make no noise about it,' the cook was saying. These girls have long tongues, and I wouldn't trust –'

She turned and saw Susan.

'If you've finished,' she said, taking the

bottle from her, 'you'd best be off to bed. You've had a long journey.'

The words were softly spoken, but they had an undertone of command. Susan took up her candlestick from the kitchen. As she passed the scullery on her way upstairs, she heard the Jarrocks whispering together and noticed, just inside the back door, two spades standing, with an empty sack beside them. They had not been there before, and she wondered idly what Jarrock could be wanting with them.

She fell asleep quickly, for she was tired; but an hour or two later she woke with a start and a feeling that people were talking in the room. The rain had ceased, for through the window she could see a star shining, and the attic was lit by the diffused grayness of moonlight. Nobody was there, but the voices were no dream. She could hear their low rumble, close beside her head. She sat up and lit her candle; then slipped out of bed and crept across to the door.

The landing was empty; from the room next to her own she could hear the deep and regular snoring of the cook. She came back and stood for a moment, puzzled. In the middle of the room, she could hear nothing, but as she returned to the bed, she heard the voices again, smothered, as though the speakers were at the bottom of a well. Stooping, she put her

180

ear to the empty fireplace. At once the voices became more distinct, and she realized that the great chimney was acting as a speaking tube from the room below. Mr. Wispell was talking. '. . . better be getting on with it . . . here at any time . . .'

'The ground's soft enough.' That was Jarrock speaking. She lost a few words, and then:

'. . . bury her four feet deep, because of the rose trees.'

There came a silence. Then came the muffled echo of Mr. Wispell's great laugh; it rumbled with a goblin sound in the hollow chimney.

Susan crouched by the fireplace, feeling herself grow rigid with cold. The voices dropped to a subdued murmur. Then she heard a door shut and there was complete silence. She stretched her cramped limbs and stood a moment listening. Then, with fumbling haste she began to drag on her clothes. She must get out of this horrible house.

Suddenly a soft step sounded on the gravel beneath her window; it was followed by the chink of iron. Then a man's voice said: 'Here, between Betty Uprichard and Evelyn Thornton.' There followed the thick sound of a spade driven into heavy soil.

Susan stole to the window and looked out. Down below, in the moonlight, Mr. Wispell and Jarrock were digging, fast and feverishly, flinging up the soil about a shallow trench. A rose tree was lifted and laid to one side, and as she watched them, the trench deepened and widened to a sinister shape.

She huddled on the last of her clothing, pulled on her coat and hat, sought for and found the handbag that held her money and set the door gently ajar. There was no sound but the deep snoring from the next-door room.

She picked up her suitcase, which she had not unpacked before tumbling into bed. She hesitated a moment; then, as swiftly and silently as she could, she tiptoed across the landing and down the steep stair. The words of Mr. Wispell came back to her with sudden sinister import. 'I hope she won't disappear like the last one.' Had the last one, also, seen that which she was not meant to see, and scuttled on trembling feet down the stair with its twisted black banisters? Or had she disappeared still more strangely, to lie forever four feet deep under the rose trees? The old boards creaked beneath her weight; on the lower landing the door of Mr. Alistair's room stood ajar, and a faint light came from within it. Was he to be the tenant of the grave in the garden? Or was it meant for her, or for the visitor who was expected that night?

Her flickering candle flame showed her the front door chained and bolted. With a caution and control inspired by sheer terror, she pulled back the complaining bolts, lowered the chain with her hand, so that it should not jangle against the door, and turned the heavy key. The garden lay still and sodden under the moonlight. Drawing the door very gently to behind her, she stood on the threshold, free. She took a deep breath and slipped down the path as silently as a shadow.

A few yards down the hill road she came to a clump of thick bushes. Inside this she thrust the suitcase. Then, relieved of its weight, she ran. At four o'clock the next morning a young policeman was repeating a curious tale to the police sergeant at Dedcaster.

'The young woman is pretty badly frightened,' he said, 'but she tells her story straight enough. Do you think we ought to look into it?'

'Sounds queerish,' said the sergeant. 'Maybe you'd better go and have a look. Wait a minute. I'll come with you myself. They're odd people, those Wispells. Man's an artist, isn't he? Loose-living gentry they are,

183

as often as not. Get the car out, Blaycock; you can drive us.'

'What the devil is all this?' demanded Mr. Wispell. He stood upright in the light of the police lantern, leaning upon his spade, and wiped the sweat from his forehead with an earthy hand. 'Is that our girl you've got with you? What's wrong with her? Hey? Thief, hey? If you've been bagging the silver, you young besom, it'll be the worse for you.'

'This young woman's come to us with a queer tale, Mr. Wispell,' said the sergeant. 'I'd like to know what you're a-digging of here for.'

Mr. Wispell laughed. 'Of here for? What should I be digging of here for? Can't I dig in my own garden without your damned interference.'

'Now, that won't work, Mr. Wispell. That's a grave, that is. People don't dig graves in their gardens in the middle of the night for fun. I want that there grave opened. What've you got inside it? Now, be careful.'

'There's nobody inside it at the moment,' said Mr. Wispell, 'and I should be obliged if you'd make rather less noise. My wife's in a delicate state of health, and my brother-in-law, who is an invalid with an injured spine, has had a very bad turn. We've had to keep

184

him under morphia and we've only just got him off into a natural sleep. And now you come bellowing round –'

'What's that there in that sack?' interrupted the young policeman. As they all pressed forward to look, he found Susan beside him, and reassured her with a friendly pat on the arm.

'That?' Mr. Wispell laughed again. 'That's Helen. Don't damage her, I implore you – if my aunt –'

The sergeant had bent down and slit open the sacking with a penknife. Soiled and stained, the pale face of a woman glimmered up at him. There was earth in her eyelids.

'Marble!' said the sergeant. 'Well, I'll be hanged!'

There was the sound of a car stopped at the gate.

'Heaven almighty!' ejaculated Mr. Wispell. 'We're done for! Get this into the house quickly, Jarrock.'

'Wait a bit, sir. What I want to know –'

Steps sounded on the gravel. Mr. Wispell flung his hands to heaven. 'Too late!' he groaned.

An elderly lady, very tall and upright, was coming round the side of the house.

'What on earth are you up to out here, Walter?' she demanded in a piercing voice.

185

'Policemen? A nice welcome for your aunt, I must say. And what – *what* is my wedding present doing in the garden?' she added, as her eye fell on the naked marble figure.

'Oh, Lor'!' said Mr. Wispell. He flung down the spade and stalked away into the house.

'I'm afraid,' said Mrs. Wispell, 'you will have to take your month's money and go, Susan. Mr. Wispell is very much annoyed. You see, it was such a hideous statue, he wouldn't have it in the house, and nobody would buy it, and besides, Mrs. Glassover might turn up at any time, so we buried it and when she wired, of course, we had to dig it up. But I'm afraid Mrs. Glassover will never forgive Walter, and she's sure to alter her will and – well, he's very angry, and really I don't know how you could be so silly.'

'I'm sure I'm very sorry, madam. I was a bit nervous, somehow –'

'Maybe,' said Mrs. Jarrock in her hoarse voice, 'the poor girl was upset-like, by Jarrock. I did ought to have explained about him and poor Mr. Alistair getting blown up in the war and you being so kind to us – but there! Being used to the poor face myself I didn't think, somehow –

and what with being all upset and one thing and another . . .'

The voice of Mr. Wispell came booming down the staircase. 'Has that fool of a girl cleared off?'

The young policeman took Susan by the arm. He had pleasant brown eyes and curly hair, and his voice was friendly.

'Seems to me, miss,' he said, 'Scrawns ain't no place for you. You'd better come along of us and eat your dinner with Mother and me.'

MARY ROBERTS RINEHART

Louise Baring in
The Lipstick

I walked home after the coroner's inquest.
Mother had gone on in the car, looking
rather sick, as indeed she had done ever since
Elinor's death. Not that she had particularly
cared for Elinor. She has a pattern of life
which divides people into conformers and
non-conformers. The conformers pay their
bills the first of the month, go to church – the
Episcopal, of course – never by any chance get
into anything but the society columns of the
newspapers, and regard marriage as the *sine
qua non* of every female over twenty.

My cousin Elinor Hammond had openly
flouted all this. She had gone gaily
through life, as if she wakened each
morning wondering what would be the
most fun that day; stretching her long
lovely body between her silk sheets –
how mother resented those sheets! – and
calling to poor tired old Fred in his
dressing room.

'Let's have some people in for cocktails, Fred.'

'Anything you say, darling.'

It was always like that. Anything Elinor said was all right with Fred. He worshipped her. As I walked home that day I was remembering his face at the inquest. He had looked dazed.

'You know of no reason why your – why Mrs. Hammond should take her own life?'

'None whatever.'

'There was nothing in her state of health to have caused her anxiety?'

'Nothing. She had always seemed to be in perfect health.'

'She was consulting Doctor Barclay.'

'She was tired. She was doing too much,' he said unhappily.

Yet there it was. Elinor had either fallen or jumped from that tenth-floor window of Doctor Barclay's waiting room, and the coroner plainly believed she had jumped. The doctor had not seen her at all that day. Only the nurse.

'There was no one else in the reception room,' she testified. 'The doctor was busy with a patient. Mrs. Hammond sat down by the window and took off her hat. Then she lit a cigarette and picked up a magazine. After

189

that I went back to my office to copy some records. I didn't see her again until –'

She was a pretty little thing. She looked pale.

'Tell us what happened next,' said the coroner gently.

'I heard the other patient leave about five minutes later. She went out from the consulting room. There's a door there into the hall. We have that arrangement, so – well, so that patients don't meet. When he buzzed for the next case, I went in to get Mrs. Hammond. She wasn't there. I saw her hat, but her bag was gone. I thought she had gone to the lavatory. Then –' She stopped and gulped. 'Then I heard people shouting in the street and I looked out the window.'

The coroner gave her a little time. She got out a handkerchief and dabbed at her eyes.

'What would you say was her mental condition that morning, Miss Comings? Was she depressed?'

'I thought she seemed very cheerful,' she said.

'The window was open beside her?'

'Yes. I couldn't believe it until I –'

He excused her then. She was openly crying by that time, and it was clear that she had told all she knew.

When Doctor Barclay was called – he had

come in late – I was surprised. I had expected an elderly man, but he was only in the late thirties and quite good-looking. Knowing Elinor, I wondered. She had had a passion for handsome men, except for Fred, who had no looks whatever. Beside me I heard mother give a ladylike snort.

'So that's it!' she said. 'She had as much need for a psychiatrist as I need a third leg.'

But the doctor added little to what we already knew. He had not seen Elinor at all that morning. When he rang the buzzer and nobody came he had gone forward to the reception room. Miss Comings was leaning out the window. All at once she began to scream. Fortunately a Mrs. Thompson arrived at that time and took charge of her. He had gone down to the street, but the ambulance had already arrived.

He was frank enough up to that time. Queried about the reason for Elinor's consulting him, he tightened, however.

'I have many patients like Mrs. Hammond,' he said. 'Women who live on their nerves. Mrs. Hammond had been doing that for years.'

'That is all? She mentioned no particular trouble?'

He smiled faintly.

'We all have troubles,' he said. 'Some we

191

imagine, some we magnify, some are real. But I would say that Mrs. Hammond was an unusually normal person. I had recommended that she go away for a rest. I believe she meant to do so.'

His voice was clipped and professional. If Elinor had been attracted to him it had been apparently a one-sided affair. Fred, however, was watching him intently.

'You did not gather that she contemplated suicide?'

'No. Not at any time.'

That is all they got out of him. He evaded them on anything Elinor had imagined, or magnified. In fact he did as fine a piece of dodging as I have ever seen. His relations with his patients, he said, were particularly confidential. If he knew anything of value he would tell it, but he did not.

Mother nudged me as he finished.

'Probably in love with her,' she said. 'He's had a shock. That's certain.'

He sat down near us, and I watched him. I saw him reach for a cigarette, then abandon the idea, and I saw him more or less come to attention when the next witness was called. It was the Mrs. Thompson who had looked after the nurse, and she was a strangely incongruous figure in that group of Elinor's family and friends. She was a large motherly-looking

192

woman, perspiring freely and fanning herself with a small folding fan.

She stated at once that she was not a patient.

'I clean his apartment for him once a week,' she said. 'He has a Jap, but he's no cleaner. That day I needed a little money in advance, so I went to see him.'

She had not entered the office at once. She had looked in and seen Elinor, so she had waited in the hall, where there was a breeze. She had seen the last patient, a woman, leave by the consulting-room door and go down in the elevator. A minute or so later she heard the nurse scream.

'She was leaning out of the window yelling her head off,' she said. 'Then the doctor ran in and we got her on a couch. She said somebody had fallen out, but she didn't say who it was.'

Asked how long she had been in the hall, she thought about a quarter of an hour. She was certain no other patient had entered during that time. She would have seen them if they had.

'You are certain of that?'

'Well, I was waiting my chance to see the doctor. I was watching pretty close. and I was never more than a few feet from the door.'

'You found something belonging to Mrs.

Hammond, didn't you?' In the office?'

'Yes, sir. I found her bag.'

The bag, it seemed, had been behind the radiator in front of the window.

'I thought myself it was a queer place for it, if she was going to – do what she did.' And she added naively, 'I gave it to the police when they came.'

So that was that. Elinor, having put her hat on the table, had dropped her bag behind the radiator before she jumped. Somehow it didn't make sense to me, and later on, of course, it made no sense at all.

The verdict was of suicide while of unsound mind. The window had been examined, but there was the radiator in front of it, and the general opinion seemed to be that a fall would have to be ruled out. Nobody of course mentioned murder. In the face of Mrs. Thompson's testimony it looked impossible. Fred listened to the verdict with blank eyes. His sister, Margaret, sitting beside him and dressed in heavy mourning, picked up her bag and rose. And Doctor Barclay stared straight ahead of him as though he did not hear it. Then he got up and went out, and while I put mother in the car I saw him driving away, still with that queer fixed look on his face.

I was in a fine state of fury as I walked home. I had always liked Elinor, even when, as mother rather inelegantly said, she had snatched Fred from under my nose. As a matter of cold fact, Fred Hammond never saw me after he first met her. He had worshipped her from the start, and his white, stunned face at the inquest only added to the mystery.

The fools, I thought. As though Elinor would ever have jumped out that window. Even if she was in trouble she would never have done it that way. There were so many less horrible ways. Sleeping tablets, or Fred's automatic, or even her smart new car and carbonmonoxide gas. But I refused to believe that she had done it at all. She had never cared what people thought. I remembered almost the last time I had seen her. Somebody had given a suppressed-desire party, and Elinor had gone with a huge letter 'A' on the front of her white satin dress.

Mother nearly had a fit when she saw it.

'I trust, Elinor,' she said, 'that your scarlet letter does not mean what it appears to mean.'

Elinor had laughed.

'What do you think, Aunt Emma?' she said. 'Would you swear that never in your life –'

'That will do, Elinor,' mother said. 'Only I am glad my dear sister is not alive, to see you.'

She had been very gay that night, and she had enjoyed the little run-in with mother.

Perhaps that was one of the reasons I had liked her. She could cope with mother. She could, of course. She wasn't an only daughter, living at home and on an allowance which was threatened every now and then. And she had brought laughter and gaiety into my own small world. Even her flirtations – and she was too lovely not to have plenty of them – had been lighthearted affairs, although mother had never believed it.

She was having tea when I got home. She sat stiffly behind the tea-tray and inspected me.

'I can't see why you worry about all this, Louise. You look dreadful,' she said. 'What's done is done. After all, she led Fred a miserable life.'

'She made him happy, and now she's dead,' I said shortly. 'Also I don't believe she threw herself out that window.'

'Then she fell.'

'I don't believe that either,' I said shortly.

'Nonsense! What do you believe?'

But I had had enough. I left her there and went upstairs to my room. It wasn't necessary for mother to tell me that I looked like something any decent dog would have buried. I could see that for myself. I sat down at my toilet table and rubbed some cream into my face, but my mind was running in circles. Somebody had killed Elinor and had gotten away with it. Yet who could have hated her enough for that? A jealous wife? It was possible. She had a way of taking a woman's husband and playing around with him until she tired of him. But she had not been doing that lately. She had been, for her, rather quiet.

Plenty of people of course had not liked her. She had a way of riding roughshod over them, ignoring their most sensitive feelings or laughing at them. She never snubbed anyone. She said what she had to say, and sometimes it wasn't pleasant. Even to Fred. But he had never resented it. He was like that.

I could see the Hammond place from my window, and the thought of Fred sitting there alone was more than I could bear. Not that I had ever been in love with him, in spite of mother's hopes. I dressed and went down to dinner, but I was still out of favour. I couldn't eat, either. Luckily it was mother's bridge night, and after she and her three cronies were settled at the table I managed to slip out through the kitchen. Annie, the cook, was making sandwiches and cutting cake.

'It beats all, the way those old ladies can eat,' she said resignedly.

I told her if I was asked for to say I had gone to bed, and went out. Fred's house was only two blocks away, set in its own grounds like ours, and as I entered the driveway I saw a man standing there, looking at it. I must have surprised him, for he turned suddenly and looked at me. It was Doctor Barclay.

He didn't recognize me, however. I suppose he had not even seen me at the inquest. He touched his hat and went out to the street, and a moment later I heard his car start off. But if he had been in the house Fred did not mention it. I rang and he himself opened the door. He seemed relieved when he saw me.

'I thought you were the damned police again,' he said. 'Come in. I've sent the servants to bed. They're all pretty well shot.'

We went into the library. It looked as if it hadn't been dusted for a month. Elinor's house had always looked that way; full of people and cigarette smoke and used highball-glasses. But at least it had looked alive. Now – well, now it didn't. So it was a surprise to see her bag lying on the table. Fred saw me looking at it.

'Police returned it today,' he said. 'Want a drink?'

'I'll have some White Rock. May I look inside it, Fred?'

'Go to it,' he said dully. 'There's nothing there that doesn't belong. No note, if that's what you mean.'

I opened the bag. It was crammed as usual: compact, rouge, coin purse, a zipper compartment with some bills in it, a small memorandum book, a handkerchief smeared with lipstick, a tiny perfume vial, and some samples of dress material with a card pinned to them. 'Match slippers to these.' Fred was watching me over his glass, his eyes red and sunken.

'I told you. Nothing.'

I searched the bag again, but I could not find the one thing which should have been there. I closed the bag and put it back on the table. But he wasn't paying any attention to me anyhow. He was staring at a photograph of Elinor in a silver frame, on the desk.

'All this police stuff,' he said. 'Why can't they just let her rest? She's asleep now, and she never got enough sleep. She was beautiful, wasn't she, Lou?'

'She was indeed,' I said honestly.

'People said things. Margaret thought she was foolish and extravagant.' He glanced at the desk in the corner, piled high with what looked like unopened bills. 'Maybe she was, but what the hell did I care?'

He seemed to expect some comment, watching me out of haggard eyes. So I said:

'You didn't have to buy her, Fred, You had her. She was devoted to you.'

He gave me a faint smile, like a frightened small boy who has been reassured.

'She was, you know, Lou,' he said. 'I wasn't only her husband. I was her father too. She told me everything. Why she had to go to that damned doctor –'

'Didn't you know she was going, Fred?'

'Not until I found a bill from him,' he said grimly. 'I told her I could prescribe a rest for her, instead of her sitting for hours with that young puppy. But she only laughed.'

He talked on, as if he was glad of an audience. He had made her happy. She went her own way sometimes, but she always came back to him. He considered the coroner's verdict an outrage. 'She fell. She was always reckless about heights.' And he had made no plans, except that Margaret was coming to stay until he closed the place. And as if the mere mention of her had summoned her, at that minute Margaret walked in.

I had never liked Margaret Hammond. She was a tall angular woman, older than Fred, and she merely nodded to me.

'I decided to come tonight,' she said. 'I don't like your being alone. And tomorrow I want to inventory the house. I'd like to have father's portrait, Fred.'

He winced at that. There had been a long quarrel about old Joe Hammond's portrait ever since Fred's marriage. Not that Elinor had cared about it, but because Margaret had always wanted it she had held onto it. I looked at Margaret. Perhaps she was the nearest to a real enemy Elinor had ever had. She had hated the marriage, had resented Elinor's easy-going extravagant life. Even now she could not help looking at the desk, piled high with bills.

'I'd better straighten that for you,' she said. 'We'll have to find out how you stand.'

'I know how I stand.'

He got up and they confronted each other, Fred with his back to the desk, as if even then he was protecting Elinor from Margaret's prying eyes.

She shrugged and let it go. Yet as I left the house I was fairly confident she would spend the night at that desk. Fred asleep, the exhausted sleep of fatigue and escape, and Margaret creeping down to the desk, perhaps finding that bill of Doctor Barclay's and showing it to him in the morning.

'So that's how she put in her time! And you pay for it!'

It was warm that night. I walked slowly home, hoping the bridge game was not over. But it seemed my night for unexpected encounters, for I had gone nearly half the way when I realized I was being followed.

That is, someone was walking softly behind me. I felt the hair rising on my scalp as I stopped and turned. But it was only a girl. When I stopped she stopped too. Then she came on, and spoke my name.

'You're Miss Baring, aren't you?'

'Yes. You scared me half to death.'

'I'm sorry. I saw you coming out of the inquest today, and a reporter told me your name. You've been to the Hammond's, haven't you?'

'Yes. What about it?'

She seemed uncertain. She stood still, fiddling with her handbag. She was quite young, and definitely uneasy.

'Were you a friend of Mrs. Hammond's?' She inquired.

'She was my cousin. Why?'

She seemed to make a decision, although she took her time to do it. She opened her bag, got out a cigarette and lit it before she answered.

'Because I think she was pushed out that window,' she said defiantly. 'I'm in an office across the street, and I was looking out. I didn't know who she was, of course.'

'Do you mean that you saw it happen?' I said incredulously.

'No. But I saw her at the window, just before it happened, and she was using a lipstick. When I looked out again she was – she was on the pavement.' She shivered, and threw away the cigarette. 'I don't think a woman would use a lipstick just before she was going to do a thing like that, do you?'

'No,' I said. 'How long was it between that and when you saw her, down below?'

'Hardly a minute.'

'You're sure it was Mrs. Hammond?'

'Yes. She had on a green dress, and I noticed her hair. She didn't have a hat on. I – well, I went back tonight to see if the lipstick was somewhere on the pavement. I couldn't find it. The street was crowded. Anyhow someone may have picked it up. It's three days ago. But I'm pretty sure she still had it when she fell.'

That was what I had not told Fred, that Elinor's gold lipstick was missing from her bag.

I looked at my watch. It was only eleven o'clock, and mother was good for another hour.

'We might go and and look again,' I said. 'Do you mind?'

She didn't mind. She was a quiet-spoken girl, certain that Elinor had not killed herself. But she didn't want her name used. In fact, she would not tell me her name.

'Just call me Smith,' she said. 'I don't

want any part of this. I've got a job to hold.'

I never saw her again, and unless she reads this she will probably never know that she took the first step that solved the case. Because I found the lipstick that night. It was in the gutter, and a dozen cars must have run over it. It was crushed flat, but after I had wiped the mud off Elinor's monogram was perfectly readable.

Miss Smith saw it and gasped.

'So I was right,' she said.

The next minute she had hailed a bus and got on it, and as I say I have never seen her since.

I slept badly that night. I heard the party below breaking up and the cars driving away. When mother came upstairs she opened my door, but I turned off the light and closed my eyes, which was the only escape I knew of. I knew then that I had a murder to consider, and it seemed unimportant whether she had won two dollars or lost it that evening. But I got up after she had settled down for the night, and hid that battered lipstick in the lining of my hatbox.

It was late when I got to Doctor Barclay's office the next morning. The reception-room door was unlocked and I walked in. The room was empty, so I went to the window and looked down. I tried to think that I was going to jump, and whether I would use a lipstick or not if I were. It only made me dizzy and weak in the knees, however, and when the nurse came in I felt like holding onto her.

If she recognized me she gave no sign of it.

'I don't think you have an appointment, have you?' she inquired.

'No. I'm sorry. Should I?'

She looked as though I had committed *lèse-majesté;* and when I gave my name she seemed even more suspicious. She agreed, however, to tell Doctor Barclay I was there, and after a short wait she took me back to the consulting-room.

The doctor got up when he saw me, and I merely put Elinor's lipstick on the desk in front of him and sat down.

'I don't think I understand,' he said, staring at it.

'Mrs. Hammond was at the window in your reception room, using that lipstick, only a minute before she fell.'

'I see.' He looked at it again. 'I suppose you mean it fell with her.'

'I mean that she never killed herself, doctor. Do you think a woman would rouge her mouth just before she meant to do – what we're supposed to think she did?'

He smiled wryly.

My dear girl,' he said, 'if you saw as
much of human nature as I do that wouldn't
surprise you.'

'So Elinor Hammond jumped out your
window with a lipstick in her hand, and
you watch the Hammond house last night
and then make a bolt for it when I appear.
If that makes sense –'

It shocked him. He hadn't recognized me
before. He leaned back in his chair and looked
at me as if he was seeing me for the first time.

'I see,' he said. 'So it was you in the
driveway.'

'It was indeed.'

He seemed to come to a decision then. He
leaned forward in his chair.

'I suppose I'd better tell you, and trust you
to keep it to yourself. I hadn't liked the way
Mr. Hammond looked at the inquest. That
sort of thing is my business. I was afraid he
might – well, put a bullet through his head.'

'You couldn't stop it, standing in the
driveway,' I said sceptically.

He laughed a little at that. It made him look
less professional, more like a human being.
Then he sobered.

'I see,' he said. 'Well, Miss Baring,
whatever happened to Mrs. Hammond, I
assure you I didn't do it. As for being
outside the house, I've told you the truth. I

was wondering how to get in when you came. His sister had called me up. She was worried.'

'I wouldn't rely too much on what Margaret Hammond says. She hated Elinor like poison.'

I got up on that and retrieved the lipstick. He got up too, and surveyed me unsmilingly.

'You're a very young and attractive woman, Miss Baring. Why don't you let this drop? After all you can't bring her back. You know that.'

'I know she never killed herself,' I said stubbornly, and went out.

I was less surprised than I might have been to find Margaret in the reception room when I reached it. She was standing close to the open window from which Elinor had fallen, and for one awful minute I thought she was going to jump herself.

'Margaret!' I said sharply.

She jerked and turned. She never used make-up, and her face was a dead white. But I was surprised to find her looking absolutely terrified when she saw me. She pulled herself together, however.

'Oh, it's you, Louise,' she said. 'You frightened me.' She sat down abruptly and wiped her face with her handkerchief. 'She must have slipped, Lou. It would be easy. Try it yourself.'

But I shook my head. I had no intention of

leaning out that window. Not with Margaret behind me. She said she had come to pay Fred's bill for Elinor, and I let it go at that. Nevertheless, there was something queer about her that day, and I felt shivery as I went down in the elevator. Women at her time of life sometimes go off-balance to the point of insanity.

I had some trouble in starting my car, which is how I happened to see her when she came out of the building. And then she did something that made me stop and watch her. There was no question about it. She was looking over the pavement and in the gutter. So she knew Elinor's lipstick had fallen with her. Either that or she had missed it out of the bag.

She didn't see me. She hailed a taxi and got into it, her tall figure in its deep mourning conspicuous in that summer crowd of thin light dresses. To this day I don't know why I followed her, except that she was the only suspect I had. Not that I really believed then that she had killed Elinor. All I knew was that someone had done it.

I did follow her, however. The taxi went on and on. I began to feel rather silly as it passed through the business section and into the residential part of town. Here the traffic was lighter and I had to fall back. But on a thinly settled street the taxi stopped and Margaret got out. She did not see me or my car. She was looking at a frame house, set back from the street, and with a narrow porch in front of it, and as I watched her she climbed the steps and rang the bell.

She was there, inside the house, for almost an hour. I began to feel more idiotic than ever. There were so many possible reasons for her being there; reasons which had nothing to do with Elinor. But when she finally came out I sat up in amazement.

The woman seeing her off on the porch was the Mrs. Thompson of the inquest.

I stooped to fix my shoe as the taxi passed me, but I don't believe Margaret even saw the car. Nor did Mrs. Thompson. She didn't go into the house at once. Instead she sat down on the porch and fanned herself with her apron, and she was still there when I went up the steps.

She looked surprised rather than apprehensive. I don't suppose she had seen me at the inquest. She didn't move.

'I hope you're not selling anything,' she said, unpleasantly. 'If you are you needn't waste your time.'

It was impossible to connect her with crime. Any crime. By the time a woman has reached fifty what she is is written indelibly on her.

Not only on her face. On her hands, on the clothes she wears and the way she wears them. She was the sort who got up in the morning and cooked breakfast for a large family. Probably did her own washing, too. Her knuckles were large and the skin on them red, as if they were too much in hot water. But her eyes were shrewd as she surveyed me.

'I'm not selling anything,' I said. 'May I sit down and talk to you?'

'What about?' She was suspicious now. 'I've got lunch to get. The children will be coming home from school.'

She got up, and I saw I would have to be quick.

'It's about a murder,' I said shortly. 'There's such a thing as being accessory after the fact, and I think you know something you didn't tell at the Hammond inquest.'

Her florid colour faded somewhat.

'It wasn't a murder,' she said. 'The verdict –'

'I know all about that. Nevertheless, I think it was a murder. What was Mrs. Hammond's sister-in-law doing here if it wasn't?'

She looked startled, but she recovered quickly.

'I never saw her before,' she said. 'She came to thank me for my testimony. Because it showed the poor thing did it herself.'

'And to pay you for it, I suppose?'

She flushed angrily.

'Nobody paid me anything,' she said. 'And now I think you'd better go. If you think anybody can bribe me to lie you're wrong. That's all.'

She went in and slammed the door, and I drove back to town, puzzled over the whole business. Was she telling the truth? Or had there been something she had not told at the inquest? Certainly I believed that the doctor had known more than he had told. But why conceal anything? I began to feel as though there was a sort of conspiracy around me, and it was rather frightening.

I was late for lunch that day, and mother was indignant.

'I can't imagine why, with nothing to do, you are always late for meals,' she said.

'I've plenty to do, mother,' I told her. 'I've been working on Elinor's murder.'

She gave a small ladylike squeal.

'Murder?' she said. 'Of course she wasn't murdered. Who would do such a thing?'

'Well, Margaret for one. She always loathed her.'

'Women in Margaret's position in life do not commit crimes,' she said pontifically. 'Really I don't know what has happened

211

to you, Louise. The idea of suspecting your friends –'

'She is no friend of mine. And Elinor was.'

'So you'll stir up all sorts of scandal. Murder indeed! I warn you, Louise, if you keep on with this idiotic idea you will find yourself spread all over the newspapers. And I shall definitely stop your allowance.'

With this dire threat she departed, and I spent the afternoon wondering what Doctor Barclay and the Thompson woman either knew or suspected, and in getting a shampoo and wave at Elinor's hairdresser's.

The girls there were more than willing to talk about her, and the one who set my hair told me something I hadn't known.

'Here I was, waiting for her,' she said. 'And she was always so prompt. Of course she never came, and –'

'You mean you expected her here, the day it happened?'

'That's right,' she agreed. 'She had an appointment for four o'clock. When I got the paper on my way home I simply couldn't believe it. She'd always been so gay. Of course the last few weeks she hadn't been quite the same, but naturally I never dreamed –'

'How long since you noticed a change in her?' I asked.

'Well, let me see. About Easter, I think. I

remember I liked a new hat she had, and she gave it to me then and there! Walked out in her bare head. I ran after her with it, but she wouldn't take it back. She said a funny thing, now I think of it. She said sometimes new hats were dangerous!'

I may have looked better when I left the shop, but what I call my mind was doing pinwheels. Why were new hats dangerous? And why had Elinor changed since Easter?

Fred had dinner with us that evening. At least he sat at the table and pushed his food around with a fork. Margaret hadn't come. He said she was in bed with a headache, and he spent most of the time talking about Elinor.

It was ghastly, of course. Even mother looked unhappy.

'I wish you'd eat something, Fred,' she said. 'Try to forget the whole thing. It doesn't do any good to go over and over it. You made her very happy. Always remember that.'

Some time during the meal I asked him if anything had happened to upset Elinor in the spring. He stared at me.

'In the spring? When?'

'About Easter?' I said. 'I thought she'd been different after that. As if she wasn't well, or something.'

'Easter?' he said. 'I don't remember

213

anything, Lou. Except that she started going to that damned psychiatrist about then.'

'Why did she go to him, Fred?' mother inquired. 'If she had any inhibitions I never noticed them.'

If there was a barb in this he didn't notice it. He gave up all pretension of eating and lit a cigarette.

'You saw him,' he said. 'He was a good-looking devil. Maybe she liked to look at him. It would be a change from looking at me.'

He went home soon after that. I thought, in spite of his previous protests, that he had resented the doctor's good looks and Elinor's visits to him. And I wondered if he was trying to build up a defence against her in his own mind; to remember her as less than perfect in order to ease his tragic sense of loss.

I slept badly. I kept seeing Fred's face, and so I was late for breakfast the next morning. Yes, we still go down to breakfast. Mother believes in the smiling morning face over the coffee cups, and the only reason I had once contemplated marrying Fred was to have a tray in bed. But at least she had finished the paper, and I took it.

Tucked away on a back page, only a paragraph or two, was an item reporting that Mrs. Thompson had been shot the night before!

I couldn't believe it.

I read and re-read it. She was not dead, but her condition was critical. All the police had been able to learn from the family was that she had been sitting alone on the front porch when it happened. Nobody had even heard the shot, or if they did they had thought it was the usual backfire. She had been found by her husband lying on the porch floor when he came home from a lodge meeting. That had been at eleven o'clock. She was unconscious when he found her, and the hospital reported her as being still too low to make a statement. She had been shot through the chest.

So she had known something, poor thing. Something that made her dangerous. And again I remembered Margaret, going up the steps of the little house on Charles Street. Margaret searching for Elinor's lipstick in the street, Margaret who had hated Elinor, and who was now in safe possession of Fred, of old Joe Hammond's portrait, of Elinor's silk sheets, and – I suddenly remembered – of Fred's automatic, which had lain in his desk drawer for years on end.

I think it was the automatic which finally decided me. That and Mrs. Thompson, hurt and perhaps dying. She had looked so – well, so motherly, sitting on that little porch of hers, with children's dresses drying on a line in the side yard, and her hands swollen with hard work. She had needed some money in advance, she had gone to the doctor's office to get it, and something had happened there that she either knew all the time, or had remembered later.

Anyhow I went to our local precinct station-house that afternoon, and asked a man behind a high desk to tell me who was in charge. He was eating an apple, and he kept on eating it.

'What's it about?' he said, eyeing me indifferently.

'It's a private matter.'

'He's busy.'

'All right,' I said. 'If he's too busy to look into a murder, then I'll go downtown to Headquarters.'

He looked only mildly interested.

'Who's been murdered?'

'I'll tell *him* that.'

There was an officer passing, and he called him.

'Young lady here's got a murder on her mind,' he said. 'Might see if the captain's busy.'

The captain was not busy, but he wasn't interested either. When I told him it was about Elinor Hammond, he said he understood the case was closed, and anyhow it

216

hadn't happened in his district. As Mrs. Thompson was not in his district either, and as he plainly thought I was either out of my mind or looking for publicity, I finally gave up. The man behind the desk grinned at me when I passed him on the way out.

'Want us to call for the corpse?' he inquired.

'I wouldn't ask you to call for a dead dog,' I told him bitterly.

But there was a result, after all. I drove around the rest of the afternoon, trying to decide what to do. When I got home I found mother in the hall, looking completely outraged.

'There's a policeman here to see you,' she hissed. 'What on earth have you done?'

'Where is he?'

'In the living-room.'

'I want to see him alone, mother,' I said. 'I haven't done anything. It's about Elinor.'

'I think you're crazy,' she said furiously. 'It's all over. She got into trouble and killed herself. She was always headed for trouble. The first thing you know you'll be arrested yourself.'

I couldn't keep her out. She followed me into the room, and before I could speak to the detective there she told him I had been acting strangely for the past few days, and

217

that she was going to call a doctor and put me to bed. He smiled at that. He was a capable-looking man, and he more or less brushed her off.

'Suppose we let her talk for herself,' he said. 'She looks quite able to. Now, Miss Baring, what's all this about a murder?'

So I told him, with mother breaking in every now and then to protest; about Elinor and the lipstick, about her appointment at her hairdresser's shortly after the time she was lying dead on the pavement, and my own conviction that Mrs. Thompson knew something she hadn't told.

'I gather you think Mrs. Hammond didn't kill herself. Is that it?'

'Does it look like it?' I demanded.

'Then who did it?'

'I think it was her sister-in-law.'

Mother almost had a fit at that. She got up, saying she had heard enough nonsense, and that I was hysterical. But the detective did not move.

'Let her alone,' he said gruffly. 'What about this sister-in-law?'

'I found her in Doctor Barclay's office yesterday,' I said. 'She insisted that Elinor had fallen out of the window. She said the floor was slippery, and she wanted me to try it myself.' I lit a cigarette, and found

218

to my surprise that my hands were shaking. 'Maybe it sounds silly, but she knew about the lipstick. She tried to find it in the street.'

But it was my next statement that really made him sit up.

'I think she was in the office the day Elinor was killed,' I said. 'I think the Thompson woman knew it. And I think she went out there last night and shot her.'

'Shot her?' he said sharply. 'Is that the woman out on Charles Street? In the hospital now?'

'Yes.'

He eyed me steadily.

'Why do you think Miss Hammond shot her?' he said. 'After all that's a pretty broad statement.'

'Because she went there yesterday morning to talk to her. She was there an hour. I know. I followed her.'

Mother started again. She couldn't imagine my behaviour. I had been carefully reared. She had done her best for me. And as for Margaret, she had been in bed last night with a headache. It would be easy to verify that. The servants –

He waited patiently, and then got up. His face was expressionless.

'I have a little advice for you, Miss Baring,' he said. 'Leave this to us. If you're right and there's been a murder and a try at another one, that's our job. If you're wrong no harm's been done. Not yet, anyhow.'

It was mother who went to bed that afternoon, while I waited at the telephone. And when he finally called me the news left me exactly where I had been before. Mrs. Thompson had recovered consciousness and made a statement. She did not know who shot her, or why, but she insisted that Margaret had visited her merely to thank her for her testimony, which had shown definitely that Elinor had either fallen or jumped out of the window. She had been neither given nor offered any money.

There was more to it, however. It appeared that Mrs. Thompson had been worried since the inquest and had called Margaret on the telephone to ask her if it was important. As a matter of fact, someone *had* entered the doctor's office while she was in the hall.

'But it was natural enough,' he said. 'It was the one individual nobody ever really notices. The postman.'

'The postman?' I said weakly.

'Exactly. I've talked to him. He saw Mrs. Hammond in the office that morning. He remembers her all right. She had her hat off, and she was reading a magazine.'

'Did he see Mrs. Thompson?'

'He didn't notice her, but she saw him all right.'

'So he went out last night and shot her!'

He laughed.

'He took his family to the movies last night. And remember this, Miss Baring. That shot may have been an accident. Plenty of people are carrying guns now who never did before.'

It was all very cheerio. Elinor had committed suicide and Mrs. Thompson had been shot by someone who was practising for Hitler. Only I just didn't believe it. I believed it even less after I had a visit from Doctor Barclay that night.

I had eaten dinner alone. Mother was still in bed refusing to see me, and I felt like an orphan. I was listening to the war news on the radio and wondering if I could learn enough about nursing to get away somewhere when the parlormaid showed him in. He was apparently not sure of his welcome, for he looked uncomfortable.

'I'm sorry to butt in like this,' he said. 'I won't take much of your time.'

'Then it's not a professional call?'

He looked surprised.

'Certainly not. Why?'

'Because my mother thinks I'm losing my mind,' I said rather wildly. 'Elinor Hammond is dead, so let her lie. Mrs. Thompson is

221

shot, but why worry? Remember the papers? Remember the family name! No scandal, please. No –'

'See here,' he said. 'You're in pretty bad shape, aren't you? How about going to bed? I'll talk to you later.'

'So I'm to go to bed!' I said nastily. 'That would be nice and easy, wouldn't it? Somebody is getting away with murder. Maybe two murders. and everybody tries to hush me up. Even the police!'

That jolted him.

'You've been to the police?'

'Why not? Why shouldn't the police be told? Just because you don't want it known that someone was pushed out of your office window –'

He was angry. He hadn't sat down, and I made no move to do so. We must have looked like a pair of chickens with our feathers spread ready to fight. But he tried to control himself.

'See here,' he said. 'You're dealing with things you don't understand. Good God, why can't you stay out of this case?'

'There wasn't any case until I made one,' I said furiously. 'I don't understand. Why is everybody warning me off?' I suppose I lost control then. The very way he was watching me set me off. 'How do I know you didn't do it yourself? You could have. Either you or the postman. And he was at the movies!'

'The postman!' he said, staring. 'What do you mean, the postman!'

I suppose it was his astonished face which made me laugh. I laughed and laughed. I couldn't stop. Then I was crying, too. I couldn't stop that either. I could hear myself practically screaming, and suddenly and without warning he slapped me in the face.

It jerked my head back and he had to catch me. But it stopped me all right. I pulled loose from him and told him to get out of the house. He didn't move, however. It didn't help to see that he had stopped looking angry; that in fact he seemed rather pleased with himself.

'That's the girl,' he said. 'You'd have had the neighbours in in another minute. You'd better go up to bed, and I'll send you some sleeping stuff from the drugstore.'

'I wouldn't take anything you sent me on a bet,' I said bitterly.

He ignored that. He redeemed my cigarette from where it was busily burning a hole in the carpet – good heavens! Mother! – and dropped it in an ashtray. Then to my fury he leaned down and patted me on the shoulder.

'Believe it or not,' he said. 'I didn't come here to attack you! I came to ask you not to go out alone at night, until I tell you you

223

may.' He picked up his hat. 'I mean what I'm saying,' he added. 'Don't go out of this house alone at night, Miss Baring. Any night.'

'Don't be ridiculous,' I said, still raging. 'Why shouldn't I go out at night?'

He was liking me less and less by the minute. I could see that.

'Because it may be dangerous,' he said shortly. 'And I particularly want you to keep away from the Hammond house. I mean that, and I hope you'll have sense enough to do it.'

He banged the front door when he went out, and I spent the next half hour trying to smooth the burned spot in the carpet and hating him like poison. I was still angry when the telephone rang in the hall. It was Margaret!

'I suppose we have you to thank for the police coming here tonight,' she said. 'Why in heaven's name can't you leave us alone? We're in trouble enough, without you making things worse.'

'All right,' I said recklessly. 'Now I'll ask you one. Why did you visit Mrs. Thompson yesterday morning? And who shot her last night?'

She did not reply. She gave a short gasp. Then she hung up the receiver.

It was a half hour later when the druggist's boy brought the sleeping tablets. I took them back to the kitchen and dropped them in the coal range, while Annie watched me with amazement. She was fixing mother's hot milk, I remember, and she told me that Clara, the Hammonds' cook, had been over that night.

'She says things are queer over there,' she reported. 'Someone started the furnace last night, and the house was so hot this morning you couldn't live in it.'

I didn't pay much attention. I was still pretty much shaken. Then I saw Annie look up, and Fred was standing on the kitchen porch, smiling his tired apologetic smile.

'May I come in?' he said. 'I was taking a walk and I saw the light.'

He looked better, I thought. He said Margaret was in bed, and the house was lonely. Then he asked if Annie would make him a cup of coffee.

'I don't sleep much anyhow,' he said. 'It's hard to get adjusted. And the house is hot. I've been getting rid of a lot of stuff. Burning it.'

So that explained the furnace. I hoped Annie heard it.

I walked out with him when he left, and watched him as he started home. Then I turned up the driveway again. I was near the house when it happened. I remember the shrubbery rustling, and stopping to see what was doing it. But I never heard the shot. Something hit me on the head. I fell, and after that there was a complete blackout until I heard mother's voice. I was in my own bed, with a bandage around my head and an ache in it that made me dizzy.

'I warned her,' mother was saying, in a strangled tone. 'The very idea of going out when you told her not to!'

'I did my best,' said a masculine voice. 'But you have a very stubborn daughter, Mrs. Baring.'

It was Doctor Barclay. He was standing beside the bed when I opened my eyes. I suppose I was still confused, for I remember saying feebly:

'You slapped me.'

'And a lot of good it did,' he retorted briskly. 'Now look where you are! And you're lucky to be there.'

I could see him better by that time. He looked very queer. One of his eyes was almost shut, and his collar was a wilted mess around his neck. I stared at him.

'What happened?' I asked dizzily. 'You've been in a fight.'

'More or less.'

'And what's this thing on my head?'

'That,' he said, 'is what you get for disobeying orders.'

I began to remember then, the scuffling in the bushes, and something knocking me down. He reached over calmly and took my pulse.

'You've got a very pretty bullet graze on the side of your head,' he said calmly. 'Also I've had to shave off quite a bit of your hair.' I suppose I wailed at that, for he shifted from my pulse to my hand. 'Don't worry about that,' he said. 'It was very pretty hair, but it will grow again. At least thank God you're here!'

'Who did it? Who shot at me?'

'The postman, of course,' he said, and to my rage and fury went out of the room.

I slept after that. I suppose he had given me something. Anyhow it was the next morning before I heard the rest of the story. Mother had fallen for him completely, and she wouldn't let him see me until my best silk blanket cover was on the bed, and I was surrounded by baby pillows. Even then in a hand mirror I looked dreadful, with my head bandaged and my skin a sort of yellowish grey. He didn't seem to mind, however. He came in, big and smiling, with his right eye purple and completely closed by that time and told me I looked like the wrath of heaven.

'You're not looking your best yourself,' I said.

227

'Oh, that!' he observed, touching his eye gingerly. 'Your mother put a silver knife smeared with butter on it last night. Quite a person, mother. We get along fine.'

He said I was to excuse his appearance, because he hadn't been home. He had been busy all night with the police. He thought he would go there now and clean up. And with that my patience gave way completely.

'You're not moving out of this room until I know what's been going on,' I stormed. 'I'm running a fever right now, out of pure excitement.'

He put a big hand on my forehead.

'No fever, he said. 'Just your detective mind running in circles. All right. Where do I start?'

'With the postman.'

So then he told me. Along in the spring Elinor had come to him with a queer story. She said she was being followed. It made her nervous. In fact, she was pretty well frightened. It seemed that the man who was watching her wherever she went wore a postman's uniform. She could be having lunch at a restaurant – perhaps with what she called a man friend – and he would be outside a window. He would turn up in all sorts of places. Of course it sounded fantastic, but she swore it was true.

228

Some faint ray of intelligence came to me.

'Do you mean it was this man the Thompson woman remembered she had seen going into your office?'

'She's already identified him. The real letter carrier had been there earlier. He had seen Mrs. Hammond sitting in a chair, reading a magazine. But he had gone before the Thompson woman arrived. The one she saw was the one who – well, the one who killed Elinor.'

I think I knew before he told me. I know I felt sick.

'It was Fred, wasn't it?'

'It was Fred Hammond. Yes.' He reached over and took my hand. 'Tough luck, my dear,' he said. 'I was worried about it. I tried to get her to go away, but you knew her. She wouldn't do it. And then not long ago she wore a dress at a party with the scarlet letter 'A' on it, and I suppose that finished him.'

'It's crazy,' I gasped. 'He adored her.'

'He had a obsession about her. He loved her, yes. But he was afraid he might lose her. Was losing her. And he was wildly jealous of her.' He looked slightly embarrassed. 'I think now he was particularly jealous of me.'

'But if he really loved her –'

'The line between love and hate is pretty fine. And it's just possible too that he felt she was never really his until – well until no one else could have her.'

'So he killed her!'

'He killed her,' he said slowly. 'He knew that nobody notices the postman, so he walked into my office and –'

He got up and went to the window. I sat up dizzily in bed.

'But he was insane,' I said. 'You can't send him to the chair.'

'Nobody will send him to the chair,' he said sombrely. 'Just remember this, my dear. He's better off where he is. Perhaps he has found his wife by this time. I think he hoped that.' He hesitated. 'I was too late last night. I caught him just in time when he fired at you, but he put up a real battle. He got loose somehow and shot himself.'

He went on quietly. There was no question of Fred's guilt, he said. Mrs. Thompson in the hospital had identified his photograph as that of the postman she had seen going into the office, and coming out shortly before she heard the nurse screaming. The bullet with which she had been shot came from Fred's gun. And Margaret – poor Margaret – had been suspicious of his sanity for a long time.'

'She came to see me yesterday after she learned the Thompson woman had been shot. She wanted him committed to an institution, but she got hysterical when I mentioned the police. I suppose there wasn't much of a case, anyhow. With Mrs. Thompson apparently dying and the uniform gone –'

'Gone? Gone how?'

'He'd burned it in the furnace. We found some charred buttons and things last night.'

I lay still, trying to think.

'Why did he try to kill Mrs. Thompson?' I asked. 'What did she know?'

'She had not only remembered seeing a postman going in and out of my office just before Miss Comings screamed. She even described him. And Margaret went home and searched the house. She found the uniform in a trunk in the attic. She knew then.

'She collapsed. She couldn't face Fred. She locked herself in her room, trying to think what to do. But she had told Fred she was going to see Mrs. Thompson that day and she thinks perhaps he knew she had found the uniform. Something might have been disturbed. She doesn't know, nor do I. All we do know is that he left this house that night, got out his car, and tried to kill the only witness against him. Except you, of course.'

'Except me!' I said.

'Except you,' he repeated dryliy. 'I tried to warn you, you may remember! I came here and you threw me out.'

'But why me? He had always liked me. Why should he try to kill me?'

'Because you wouldn't leave things alone,' he said. 'Because you were a danger from the minute you insisted Elinor had been murdered. And because you telephoned Margaret last night and asked her why she had visited Mrs. Thompson, and who had shot her.'

'You think he was listening in?'

'I know he was listening in. He wasn't afraid of his sister. She would have died to protect him, and he knew it. But here you were, a child with a stick of dynamite, and you come out with a thing like that! That was when Margaret sent me to warn you.'

I suppose I flushed.

'I'm sorry,' I said guiltily. 'I've been a fool all along, of course.'

His one remaining eye twinkled.

'I wouldn't go as far as that,' he said. 'That stubbornness of yours really broke the case. Not,' he added, 'that I like stubborn women. Gentle and mild is my motto.'

I had difficulty in getting him back to the night before. He seemed to want to forget it. But he finally admitted that he had been watching the Hammond house all evening, and that when Fred came to our kitchen door he had been just outside. Fred however had

232

seemed quiet. He drank his coffee and lit a cigarette. And then of course I had walked out to the street with him.

'Good God,' he said. 'If ever I wanted to waylay anyone and beat her up –'

However it had looked all right at first. Fred had started down the street towards home, and he followed him behind the hedge. But just too late he lost him, and he knew he was on his way back. Fred had his revolver lifted to shoot me when he grabbed him.

Suddenly I found I was crying. It was all horrible. Elinor at the window, and Fred behind her. Mrs. Thompson, resting after a hard day's work, and Fred shooting her. And I myself –

He got out a grimy handkerchief and dried my eyes.

'Stop it,' he said. 'It's all over now, and you're a very plucky young woman, Louise Baring. Don't spoil the record.'

He got up rather abruptly.

'I think you've had enough of murder and sudden death,' he said lightly. 'What you need is quiet. I'm giving up your case, you know. There will be someone in soon to dress that head of yours.'

'Why can't you do it?'

'I'm not that sort of doctor.'

I looked up at him. He was haggard and

tight with strain. He was dirty, he needed a shave, and that awful eye of his was getting blacker by the minute. But he was big and strong and sane. A woman would be safe with him, I thought. Any woman. Although of course she could never tell him her dreams.

'I don't see why you can't look after me,' I said. 'If I'm to look bald I'd prefer you to see it. After all you did it.'

He grinned. Then to my surprise he leaned down and kissed me lightly on the cheek.

'I've wanted to do that ever since you slammed that lipstick down in front of me,' he said. 'And now for God's sake will you stop being a detective and concentrate on growing some hair on the side of your head? Because I'm going to be right around for a considerable time.'

When I looked up mother was in the doorway, beaming.

ACKNOWLEDGEMENTS

'The Lover of St Lys' by F. Tennyson Jesse, from *The Premiere Magazine* (1918), copyright © 1918 by F. Tennyson Jesse, copyright © 1989 by The Harwood Will Trust; reprinted by permission of Mrs Joanna Colenbrander for the Public Trustee – Harwood Will Trust.

'Tape-Measure Murder' by Agatha Christie, from *Three Blind Mice and Other Stories* (1950), copyright © 1934 by Agatha Christie, renewed 1961 by Agatha Christie Mallowan; reprinted by permission of Aitken & Stone Ltd.

'The Mackenzie Case' by Viola Brothers Shaw, from *Mystery League Magazine* (1934).

'Easter Devil' by Mignon G. Eberhart, from *The Cases of Susan Dare*, copyright © 1934 by Mignon G. Eberhart, copyright renewed © 1962 by Mignon G. Eberhart; reprinted by permission of Brandt & Brandt Literary Agents, Inc.

'The Gilded Pupil' by Ethel Lina White, from *Detective Stories of Today* (London: Faber & Faber Ltd, 1940).

'Scrawns' by Dorothy L. Sayers reprinted by permission of David Higham Associates Limited.

235

'The Lipstick' by Mary Roberts Rinehart, from *The Complete Murder Sampler* (London: Macdonald, 1950).

The publishers hope that this book has given you enjoyable reading. Large Print Books are specially designed to be as easy to see and hold as possible. If you wish a complete list of our books, please ask at your local library or write directly to: Curley Publishing, Inc., P.O. Box 37, South Yarmouth, Massachusetts, 02664.